SOCCER COACHING THE EUROPEAN WAY

Also by Eric G. Batty

Soccer Coaching: The Modern Way
International Football Book (editor)

SOCCER COACHING THE EUROPEAN WAY

edited by
ERIC G. BATTY

The Dial Press
New York

Published by
The Dial Press
1 Dag Hammarskjold Plaza
New York, New York 10017

This work was first published in Great Britain by Souvenir Press Ltd.

Manufactured in the United States of America

First U.S.A. Printing

Library of Congress Cataloging in Publication Data

Soccer coaching the European way.

    1. Soccer—Coaching—Addresses, Essays, Lectures
I. Batty, Eric G.
GV943.8.S66   796.134'07'7   80-19945
ISBN 0-8037-7874-0

CONTENTS

INTRODUCTION

All the contributors to this book were carefully chosen and they include many of the top names in the game to-day, respected coaches, known for the quality of the football their teams have produced, and backed up by their records in terms of successes achieved.

The contributors were asked to write on various topics covering the whole spectrum of the game, and were carefully selected to give as thorough and broad a view of the game as possible.

Ron Greenwood brings to the fore the essential basics of the game which so many other coaches ignore, and Frank Blunstone, the former Manchester United Youth coach, describes in great detail the next step up dealing with giving players a wide range of basic skills.

Other big names, including Hennes Weisweiler and Rinus Michels, who are probably the most widely respected coaches in continental Europe, describe in detail how they set out to achieve the superlative quality of play that was so clearly seen in Borussia Mönchengladbach and Ajax and Holland in the 1974 World Cup.

Within these pages are a wide variety of basic approaches to the problem of coaching presented by a wide variety of international experts.

This book is not intended merely for the master coaches but for the broad spectrum of coaches at every level, and even interested spectators who have a yen to understand the game better.

At whatever level a coach works, he faces the problems

of improving his players individually in terms of basic skills and both speed and stamina and all these aspects are dealt with in depth by master craftsmen.

In addition, the art of coaching is related to passing on the ideas of the coach to the players, and getting them to play the type of game that the coach has in mind. Here we have the methods, described in detail by coaches from several countries who use a different basic approach with the same end in view: to improve the play of the team as a whole.

In effect, when trying to give his ideas to players, the coach needs a vehicle on which he can convey his ideas; a method of coaching that will enable him to show how he wants his players to perform.

Thus, coaches at every level will discover in this book several different, but proven methods of coaching players collectively to produce good quality combined play, and to get the individual player thinking in terms of applying his own personal abilities within the framework of the team effort.

There is in fact something for everyone involved in the game at every level in this book. The discerning reader will pick up point after point that he has not thought of before, or perhaps felt but never been able to put into words or translate into a form that can be coached.

It must be appreciated however that asking lesser players to do exactly what the master coaches ask of their international class players would be foolish. The ideas presented in this book must be adapted to the level at which the individual coach works. Whether the coach applies an idea from this book to improve speed, skill or combined play, a start must be made at a level at which his players will be able to measure up to.

To ask players to try and do things that are beyond them will destroy confidence and perhaps even confuse.

So the coach must be careful to choose a target for his players that they can achieve. After that, step by step, if he works with his players over a long period then there is no reason why good players should not reach the level where they can train as top level players do. But the approach must be simple, and progress must be dictated by the improvement shown by the players.

Finally, I know from experience how frustrating it can be for a coach to be aware of the finer points of the game and have a deep knowledge of coaching that is beyond the capabilities of his players. But if it is a fact that there is a great deal for every coach at every level within this book that he can put to practical use at once, it will also help him to have a deeper insight into the game than ever before, and even if his players are not ready to be coached at his new high level, it will help the coach understand even better, the game in which he is passionately involved.

ERIC G. BATTY

SOCCER COACHING THE EUROPEAN WAY

1/ The Basics of the Game: Balance, Adjustment of the Feet and the Pacing of the Ball

by **Ron Greenwood**

Ron Greenwood was born in Burnley, Lancashire on 11th November 1921. While serving in the RAF he turned out as a guest player for Chelsea and signed as a professional with them in 1943.

A left half or centre half he was transferred to Bradford Park Avenue and Brentford before returning to Chelsea where he won a championship medal. He ended his active career at Fulham.

While still playing he began coaching Walthamstow Avenue, a London amateur club and was also the coach of Oxford University.

After retirement he became manager of Eastbourne and also manager-coach of the England Youth team.

In 1957 he became assistant manager at Arsenal, remaining there until appointed manager-coach of West Ham United in 1961.

During Ron Greenwood's reign at West Ham the club earned a reputation for playing good football. They won the FA Cup in 1964 and the European Cup-winners Cup in 1965, beating TSV München 1860 2–0 in a very fine final.

An outstanding coach, Ron Greenwood specialised in developing young players and amongst the best known players to benefit from his coaching were Bobby Moore, Geoff Hurst and Martin Peters who played a key role in helping England win the World Cup in 1966.

In 1977, Ron Greenwood became temporary manager of the England team, and following a convincing 2–0 victory over Italy, his position was confirmed by the Football Association early in 1978.

In his contribution Ron Greenwood draws attention to the fact that whatever skill is being performed or coached, the adjustment of the body is vital. If the body is not adjusted correctly then the skill cannot be performed with the necessary accuracy.

Drawing attention to the adjustment of the body, Ron Greenwood analyses several skills and shows that success in performing the most difficult skills depends on being correctly balanced. Thus he states, the standing foot on which the body is balanced is just as important as the foot that plays the ball because without good balance, no skill can be performed.

Progressing further, Ron Greenwood goes on to point out that when a player is able to pass first time, or score a spectacular goal with a first time shot, it was the player who gave him the pass with the right degree of pace that made it possible. Thus the pacing of the ball when passing is the key to good football.

Finally, this contribution is completed by a description of one of the simple practices which helped to enable Bobby Moore, Geoff Hurst and Martin Peters to become outstanding players and made West Ham such a good side to watch.

Many people have spoken and written of the basics of the game, starting with the performance of skills with the ball, but invariably they ignore the most basic element of all, which is the body of the player.

Practically every book ever published on football coaching begins with how to kick the ball correctly. It is explained that the non-kicking foot has to be placed alongside the ball, but after that the standing foot, as we may call it, is never referred to again.

If you think about the standing foot it will become apparent that it is this foot which takes the body weight and provides the vitally important balance. This remains true whether one refers to the simple kicking of a dead ball, or the skills that involve playing the ball when it is in the air.

Reference to the standing foot and balance leads directly to what I see as the real basic of the game, which is using the body: the standing foot, the kicking foot, the trunk and even the arms to provide balance. So it must be repeatedly emphasised how important correct adjustment of the body is, in performing the whole range of skills with the ball.

Analyse any of the difficult skills and it will become clear that the essential ingredient that any great player must have is balance.

It is relatively easy to be nicely balanced and adjust the body correctly when coaching basics. But it is far more difficult, when one thinks in terms of being nicely balanced, adjusting the body correctly, when playing a moving ball first time. This is because, while the standing foot must be in the right place to provide balance, the ball is only alongside it for a fraction of a second, and it is in that moment that the standing foot must be right, the body correctly positioned and nicely balanced. In tennis and golf, book after book is written about how to play, but in these books the emphasis is not on the ball. Everything they write about is related to the body; to having the body perfectly positioned in relation to the ball and to be well balanced.

Tennis is closer to football because the players have to deal with a moving ball. Tennis books emphasise the importance of moving the body and adjusting it so that it is correctly placed to play the ball, and to getting good balance. Without these two basic ingredients a player cannot make even the simplest shot successfully.

In football people do not write about the body because they are more concerned with other aspects like tactics etc., so we never really get down to the basic requirements of the game.

So balance is the first essential ingredient that any good player must have. In football the player is constantly in movement and frequently called upon to play the ball while moving, so to be able to play well, he must be well balanced all the time.

Many people think that a player has nice balance if he beats people with the ball, feinting and weaving, moving his body from one side to the other. A player needs good balance to be able to do that of course, but it is not balance in the way that I mean it.

To perform any skill correctly, the player must be well balanced. Balance is the basic ingredient of everything the players do with the ball from trapping to volleying.

The important point about balance is that it is how you stand on the foot that holds the body up for it is this foot that provides the necessary balance and it is this that must be emphasised to young players.

In the 1950's we used to watch visiting continental players in training and they spent a lot of time juggling with the ball, keeping it up in the air for long periods using their feet, their thighs, their chests.

But to juggle with the ball as they did, it was vital to have excellent balance for that is the basic requirement.

You must have good balance to perform any skill because the standing foot has to be continually adjusted to what is required for each skill. So juggling with the ball demands continuous movement of the feet to maintain good balance. Looking at the other side of this coin, many bad footballers are flat footed, and a flat footed player cannot adjust his feet at all. Without balance, everything is done with the body rigid and solid. This is the opposite of what is required for to perform delicate skills the player must have litheness and good balance.

Weight lifting only develops strength and does nothing for flat footed, solid and rigid players. To play good football we need players who are athletic, agile and supple, for without these qualities they cannot be well balanced and adjust their feet quickly. This is why I think that weight lifting for footballers is absolutely tragic.

If we were to pay more attention to the questions of balance and body adjustment we would help almost every player to improve. So perhaps the most important thing is to impress on both coaches and players that movement of the feet, balance, and adjustment of the body are the basic ingredients of the game. Watch an average player strike a ball and there will be no adjustment of the feet before he plays it. In this situation, THE BALL IS DICTATING TO THE PLAYER.

If a player is asked to play the ball as it comes to him in the air he just sticks up a foot and tries to strike the ball. But because he has not had the pre-meditation to move his feet his body is cramped, and the ball will fly off anywhere.

Coaches should make players aware that they have got to use their feet and adjust their bodies in every aspect of controlling the ball or kicking the ball. If they did, it would produce a tremendous improvement in playing standards at all levels.

Take as an example the skill of volleying a ball.

First the player must judge the flight of the ball and then use his feet to get his body in the right place. Now he must adjust his body so that he strikes the ball correctly.

If the player is going to volley the ball at goal with his left foot then his right shoulder should be almost touching the ground.

With his feet in the right place and nicely balanced on his right foot, he also has his body adjusted correctly to perform the skill and he can therefore expect to hit a good volley.

Francis Lee was a very good example to follow in this for he could volley the ball really well because he had good balance and a supple body.

When Lee was going to volley with his left foot he dropped his right shoulder and got his left foot up easily because his body was supple. With all the weight of his body on his right foot he had nice balance, and could get his left foot up high enough to hit a volley on a low trajectory.

When you see a volley hit on a high trajectory and the ball finishes up in the stand it is due to the fact that the body was in the wrong place or was not supple enough, or the player was not well balanced.

One day at West Ham I saw a situation that must be typical for many groups of young players. They were practising passing in a triangle about twenty yards apart and as the ball travelled to each one in turn, they were standing still and just kicking the ball with a swing of the leg. Of course they were not as accurate as they should have been.

I went over to them and explained that they had to move their bodies every time, as the ball was coming to them. They could play a ball coming straight at them with the outside of the foot or the inside of the foot, but in each case they would have to move their feet differently in order to get their bodies adjusted correctly. To play the ball with the inside of the right foot and pass it on to a

player on their left, they would have to move their feet
so that their right shoulder was pointing towards the man
who had played the ball. Then with their body correctly
adjusted and nicely balanced, they could expect to make
a good pass.

Going one step further, the players could have used
their feet in such a way that it looked as if they were going
to pass as just described, but then change their mind, re-
adjust their feet and play the ball back to the man they
received the pass from.

Because they have moved their bodies they might play
the ball with the outside of the foot, or they might step
back and adjusting their bodies again, and play it with the
inside of the foot. The options would be there all the time.

This is the very essence of the game because the ball
will be played around while the players are in movement
and it will be more realistic, because in matches no one
ever plays the ball in a triangle with everyone standing
still.

In practice, players should play the ball around in
movement just as they do in the game. But even the
majority of the great players do not have the imagination
to practise skills in movement, and do things over and
over to perfect their technique. They will only do it if the
coach explains why they should do it and supervises them.

So if the great players do not practise simple ball skills
the right way, how can you expect young boys to do it
correctly unless they are told?

If we take a simple kicking practice, I think the players
should attempt to use the whole range of their bodies, and
the coach could make them do it by asking them to volley
the ball around to each other first time.

With three players volleying the ball first-time to each
other, say, twenty or thirty or forty yards (according to
their age and kicking ability) they would have to try to

play the ball with both their left foot and their right. Having to try and play the ball first time they would now see the necessity of making their body work, and they would enjoy it because they would be testing both their bodies and their skills.

They would be working hard because sometimes, having judged the flight and pace of the ball, they would have to *run round the ball*, moving their feet and adjusting their bodies so that they could reach the ball and play it first time, and sometimes they might have to go forward or backwards in order to play it on the volley, first time.

I have found that some players (a very small, elite proportion) do move their feet and adjust their bodies quite naturally without knowing it. But here I am thinking in terms of cultivating in all players the ability to play the ball the right way and play better football.

I am not thinking now of the top class professionals but with the development of young players, to help them improve. They should concentrate on doing the things that are the basic requirements of the game, and it is the coaches that must give them the ideas and tell them that these are the important things to practise.

It is because balance and adjustment of the body is so important to the game that many people have thought that players would benefit from having dancing lessons, and even ballet has been suggested.

But there is no need for that if the coaches appreciate that everything in football is related to balance and adjustment of the body and movement of the feet, and of course pass on this awareness to their players and get them to practise all skills in such a way that these vital qualities are developed.

It is in this sense that I believe that continental European players are better adapted to the requirements of the game than the British. They have more supple bodies generally, and a more athletic approach to the game through their agility.

The British are very Nordic. Solid and strong. But that does not mean that we could not improve our agility with a more athletic approach to the game. As a race the Germans are very much like the British, but the West Germans have adopted an athletic approach to the game.

The West Germans have always made their players move by getting them to sell a dummy before they play a ball, even in ordinary practice. In this way movement becomes natural, and there is always an adjustment of the body before they even approach the ball to play it.

The Brazilians are even more athletic and supple than the West Germans, but this is not so much acquired through practice but a national characteristic.

All the great players in the world have an appreciation of how to use early (first time) balls and nine times out of ten it is in the air. So they have got to be able to play the ball early, with little controlled volleys.

First they are aware of the situation and what is required, and they have good balance. So they can put one foot up in the air at any required angle, and flick the ball over the head of an opponent.

Everyone appreciated such skills when Pelé produced them, but the whole essence of the movement is related to the fact that the player has good balance. The player is standing on one foot, and is able to stretch the other one up in the air and play the ball at around the height of his ear with a little flick.

Watching the 1976 Olympic Games soccer tournament on television, I saw players from the Sudan against the Soviet Union. The Sudanese players were kicking the ball at heights where the Russians were trying to head it but being beaten. In fact the Sudan players were using the wrong skills in relation to what was required, but this was an indication of their suppleness. With their long legs and suppleness I am sure they could perform a much greater range of skills than British players could.

What coaches have to do is make players generally more supple and more athletic. With these qualities, then, as the ball is approaching, the player will be thinking of what his body has got to do; and how and where he must position his body, in order to strike the ball properly.

Because we do not cultivate the body and our coaches do not make the players aware of what is required in terms of adjusting the body, we see as a result, a lack of skill.

Summing up, we have illustrated in a variety of ways why it is necessary for coaches to try and give their players better balance and an awareness that in every situation they must move their feet and adjust their bodies.

For the benefit of spectators who might read this, and perhaps convince any coaches who may not have been persuaded by the arguments already put forward, let me take two far more simple situations to illustrate my points.

As a team is defending, watch the goalkeeper only as he positions and re-positions following each movement of the ball. This underlines the importance of moving the feet in pre-meditation.

Then, when a shot has finally been made, note how the goalkeeper is up on his toes, nicely balanced and able to pounce to the right or left because he is well balanced.

This movement of the feet is essential to carry out any given skill in football, even heading.

When Tommy Lawton first went to Everton as a boy before World War Two, he saw Dixie Dean heading the ball at far above average heights.

Dean told Lawton "you will never be able to head the ball well until you learn to do the essential things with your feet".

What Dean meant was that it is the adjustment of the feet as the ball approaches that enables a good header of the ball to get up and eventually head it.

My comments about the body are not only relevant to British players but also those in North America and Scandinavia particularly. Having drawn attention to the body, adjustment of the feet, pre-meditation will allow a player to make the necessary physical adjustments as the ball is coming to him and we can now pass on to the ball.

Pre-meditation is not the same thing as anticipation. Pre-meditation is advance thinking of the position the body must be in to play the ball correctly, done as the ball approaches. Anticipation is a sixth sense that tells players what opponents are going to do.

With pre-meditation a good player will always be able to deal correctly with a good ball played to him. He will be in a position to dictate to the ball. Yet no matter how high the level of skill of the individual, he may suffer if the ball played to him is not correctly placed or played at the wrong pace.

So the essence of good ball control lies in the ability of the player giving the pass, and playing it at the right pace.

Very often you see a ball thumped at a player and this highlights the necessity for players to appreciate the importance of correctly pacing the ball. When a ball is really whacked at a player he has no chance to control it, no matter how quick his pre-meditation or how good his balance.

But if the pace of the ball is right, it automatically gives the recipient time to benefit from his pre-meditation, by using his feet and adjusting his body, and now the ball is playable first time.

So we must make the players acutely aware, just how vital the correct pacing of a ball is.

This can be done very simply by putting a very skilful player under pressure by having three or four players spread around him, each with a ball. In turn, the players with a ball really whack it at the player; delivering the ball at a variety of heights up his body, but though accurate passes are made to him, hit with such power that he has no chance to control the ball, because he has no time.

Now he will appreciate the essence of correct weighting of a ball or giving his passes the right pace.

The player receiving a ball must be able to dictate to the ball and play it first time if necessary, and this can only be done if the pace of the ball up to him allows him time to move his feet and adjust his body in pre-meditation and get his body sideways on to the ball.

This is a far deeper insight into how the game should be played because every ball that is playable first time, allows the player time to adjust his body. Simultaneously, as the player receiving the pass moves his feet and body in pre-meditation, he can also look around because the pace of the ball allows him the time to do so. This is true, even if the player is tightly marked—if the ball is played in short of him and he has to go to meet it. As he moves he can look around and see where everyone is.

When Stanley Matthews had the ball at his feet, he never looked at it. He felt it! And knowing where the ball was, he was able to keep his head up, looking around constantly to see where everyone was.

The same was true of Matthews even before he received the pass if it was played at the correct pace. One glance told Matthews where he had to be to meet the ball right and pre-meditation enabled him to adjust his body to receive it. Now, even as the ball was still on its way to him, Matthews had his head up with his eyes everywhere, busy taking pictures.

All this was possible simply because the purveyor of the pass gave the ball the right pace.

So the essence of good football is related to passing the ball around with the right pace, and the ball has got to be played in relation to the opponent marking the player receiving the ball, always on the wrong side for the defender.

The wrong side for a defender is the far side of the player receiving the ball so that the defender always has his opponent's body between him and the ball, thus preventing him from being able to get at it and play it.

A long ball that has been hit in the air has to be "dropped in" short of the recipient so that he can come off and control the ball, or play it away first time. And if he goes to meet the ball he can even take the ball on his chest. But this is not the type of ball that has been hit long and dropped straight onto his chest, but one that has been nicely dropped in ten yards short of him. Now the player receiving the ball can judge the pace of the ball and know where he must meet it, and he can look around as he moves to meet the ball. Compare this ball dropped in short of a centre forward with one that is just smacked up the middle with no thought. The centre forward has no idea where the ball is going, and at best will only have the chance to fight for it with his opponent.

So the purveying of the ball: the pacing of the ball and the length of the pass form a basic ingredient of good football.

When I talk to players for the first time, I make a point of telling them to "make every ball playable first time" and I know from experience that they do not even begin to understand what I mean.

The simplest way to give a player an appreciation of this vital point is to get him to perform simple skills in training.

He will find that even in this false situation in which there is no opponent on a training ground and he has only the ball to worry about, he cannot perform the skill if the ball is not played up to him just right in terms of pace. If the ball is hit too hard, then even in training the player will not be able to make a simple pass first time. This is because by hitting the ball at him hard, we give him no space to play in.

Many people talk freely about good players "making space for themselves" but there is space on a football field all the time. This is the space between two players, even if there is an opponent in the way, apparently filling that space, the ball can be played over his head and "dropped in".

So it is how the two players use this space, how the ball is purveyed between them that determines whether or not they will be able to keep possession and continue a passing movement.

So the placing of a ball up to a colleague—always on the opposite side to the defender—and the pace of the ball are vital to good football.

If the forward is going off on a run then he wants the ball played up to him just right so that it is there, rolling alongside him on the opposite side to the defender marking him. The pace of the ball is vital for it must not be hit too hard or not hard enough. The ball has to arrive exactly right, rolling nicely alongside him at the right pace, just waiting for a skill to be performed with it.

The ability to play such a ball over say twenty or thirty yards demands real ball control. For this it is essential to have a lovely feel for the ball and a sense of touch. Players who have this sense of touch and feel for the ball can make passes of all kinds, and they make it easy for the recipient to play the ball.

Thus, a nicely paced ball gives the recipient time to look

around and get "pictures". All the work has been done for him by the correct weighting of the ball played up to him.

Relative to his opponent and what he is going to do—and he knows this from his pictures—he now has a wide range of opportunities. He can come off and turn on the ball if he has time; but if he knows from his pictures that he must play the ball first time, then his pictures tell him where his colleagues are and who is best placed to pass to first time.

But all this was made possible by the right pacing of the ball up to him. So in practice the players must seek the perfection that will enable them to play every ball just right. As in all walks of life practice makes perfect.

Players like Raymond Kopa and Alfredo Di Stefano cultivated these things naturally, but I have known many players who were able to grasp the points when put to them and get great joy out of perfecting their technique. Perhaps the best known players in this category were Johnny Byrne, Martin Peters, Geoff Hurst and Bobby Moore, and they all made the game look easy. They were able to give this impression because they had acquired the necessary basic habits and had lively minds that were always taking pictures of everything around them.

The greatest of all was Alfredo Di Stefano. Wherever he was, even with the ball at the other end of the pitch, his head seemed to be on a swivel.

Di Stefano always walked on his toes, perfectly balanced, and his body was continually switching sideways to the ball while his head twitched as if he had some nervous affliction.

With his head constantly turning and switching around, Di Stefano had every picture in his mind that he could ever want. So when the ball was on its way to him he could think . . . "my options are this, and this and this" . . . and he could make his selection at once.

It was all to do with pre-meditation. He had seen the space and thought about it, and he had seen his team-mate. After that it was only a question of having the necessary skill to translate his thought into action.

Many players get better as they get older, even without good coaching. This is because these players have the capacity to think and relate their thinking to the game.

But when they reach this certain age, *when their mind is governing their bodies,* they tend not to have the necessary speed and strength to shine in competitive football.

Younger players fly about all over the place because their bodies are governing their minds instead of the reverse, and this is the tragedy of football.

If coaches can make these young players appreciate the importance of adjustment of the feet and body, of pre-meditation, and the need to pace the ball about correctly, they would improve enormously.

If coaches could also give defenders a similar appreciation of the importance of balance and movement of the feet, and if they could help them acquire a better appreciation of reading the game, then they would know that they cannot win a ball that is played up to an opponent in the right place and with the right pace, and then they will realise that all they can do is to get tight on their man and try to lock him up by placing their bodies in the way and prevent him from turning.

This would give both the attacking player and the defender the same weapons and now it would be a battle of wits between the two of them, and that is what the game is really about.

I would highlight the importance of adjusting the body and moving the feet, allied to the correct pacing of the ball with what I call third man runs, as described in Diagram 1.

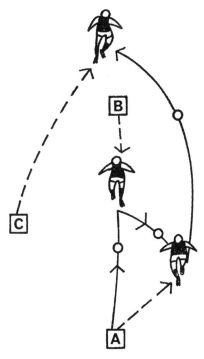

Diagram 1

Who would you think is the vital player when A sets
the ball up to B, who comes off—bringing his opponent—
and lays the ball back to be plonked in for the runner?

Everyone with the slightest knowledge of the game will
recognise the great through ball, and they will also give
credit to the runner.

But to me it is the man in the middle who is vital. He
has said to player A . . . "here I am, I have come off and
made space for the runner. Just give the ball to me and I
will lay it back for you to drop it in".

My appreciation of this situation will be borne out by
experience if you set up the practice.

Player A will be pretty accurate with his first pass, and
he will run to support all right. Player C will also make

his runs, but it will all break down if the middle man, player B, does not get everything right.

If player B does not adjust his body correctly and move his feet; if he hammers the ball back too hard to A, then it will be impossible for the through ball to be played first-time.

What player B has to do seems to be very simple, but to me, simplicity is genius, and that is what the game is all about.

If we carry this kind of assessment of what is really important into the game as a whole, see how many times in a match passing movements break down because a ball has been over-paced or under-paced, or because the ball was up in the air when it should have been on the ground or vice versa.

If player A was someone like Franz Beckenbauer or Bobby Moore you would see that he appears to have split vision, because most of the time he would not be looking at the ball. His head would be up—taking pictures

Young boys have to be told to get their heads up and look around, which many of them find very difficult. This is because someone stupidly told them to keep their eye on the ball.

If you go on any recreation ground in Britain you will see everyone chasing around, fighting for the ball. Very few will have the good basic technique that will enable them to knock the ball off, first time, with accuracy. The vast majority will be so busy trying to get the ball that when they get it they will have no pre-meditation, no pictures. So when they do get the ball they will have to look up and take a picture.

Without pre-meditation no one can play the game at a high level. The player must have pictures in his mind so that he can see to create.

A good player gets the ball and sets it up to a colleague

early, and he lays it back. Then as the ball is rolling nicely back towards him, the good player is looking all around to make his selection for a telling pass.

A good player knows from one quick glance that the ball laid back to him is just right in terms of pace, and that makes it playable first time. So now he looks up and takes up-to-date pictures. But the best players can change their minds at the very last fraction of a second, even as their foot touches the ball to play it and their heads go down to look at the ball. This is because they had not just one picture, but three or four.

Thus, if an opponent moves to cover his first selection, the good player can make an alternative choice, even as he goes to play the ball.

A simple practice will highlight many of the things mentioned, as described in Diagram 2.

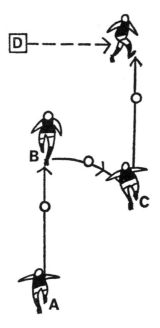

Diagram 2

Four players, two in the middle—players B and C.

Player A, at the end, starts with a pass to B who should be about thirty yards away. B plays the ball, rolling it back first time to player C.

The ball from B should be playable first time by C, so that he can hit player D at the far end, who should also be about thirty yards away.

This is a simple exercise that could be done without movement, but we want to emphasise the question of taking pictures and relating it to passing. So as the ball from B is rolling back to player C, the coach should get D to move right or left, and change his position.

After the first sequence, the ball goes back from player D up to C, who plays it back nicely to player B, who purveys it, even with his change of position, accurately to player A so that it is again playable first time.

Now we begin the passing sequence all over again from player A and repeat and keep it going, all with first time passes, and with the end men (players A and D) changing their positions after the ball has been laid back to the supporting player C or B.

Now, with movement we get this sequence: LOOK, SEE, PLAY THE BALL.

We can bring in this element into any basic skill practice, simply by adding movement. Just before the ball comes to the player practising the skill, his target has to move, but the player still has to find him. He will only be able to do this if he has his head up taking pictures, splitting his vision between the ball and his target.

Another simple practice which really brings out this look, see, play sequence, is described in Diagram 3 with four players and two balls.

The coach nominates one man, player C for example, to be the target and players A and B who start with a ball

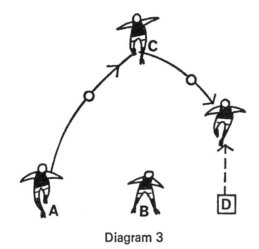

Diagram 3

each have to play the ball up to C in turn over various distances within a given area.

Player C moves around so that A and B have to play a variety of passes; long, short, on the ground and up in the air.

The task for player C who is receiving all the first passes, is to find the player without a ball and knock it off to him first time. This will be player D at the start, and the player without a ball has to move as the ball is on its way up to player C.

Every ball is played up to player C, and he has to find the free man with no ball with a first time pass.

The man with no ball has to make runs all the time to make it difficult for player C to find him. Often it will be necessary for player C to control the ball and turn before passing to the free man—if he is hiding on his blind side.

The practice can continue for any period relative to the skill of the players and the aim of course is to cultivate the ability to find a free man and play to him.

Every player in the team needs this quality so everyone should have plenty of practice at being player C.

It was with simple practices like those described that players like Moore, Peters and Hurst were brought up on, doing simple things as described. In this way they came to know, almost blindfolded, where their colleagues were (and their opponents), as they knocked the ball around.

Very simple exercises, with no opposition, but very hard to do properly as any coach will find the first time he tries them on his players.

by **Hennes Weisweiler**

Hennes Weisweiler was born at Lechenich, a suburb of Cologne on 5th December 1919, and played as a stopper centre half for 1st FC Köln and Wacker München. Like many other players of his time, the Second World War interfered with his playing career.

As a coach Hennes Weisweiler played an important part in German football as assistant to Sepp Herberger at the Cologne Sportschule from 1954 to 1969. At the same time he was coaching Viktoria Köln from 1958 to 1964, and from 1964 he took over Borussia Mönchengladbach, then unknown outside Germany.

With Borussia he steered them, first into the Bundesliga and then on to win the championship four times and estab- the club in the European Cup, well known for their attacking play.

Half his players became full internationals, headed by Berti Vogts, Gunter Netzer, Jupp Heynckes and Rainer Bonhof. The combination of players from FC Bayern München and Borussia Mönchengladbach helped Germany win the 1974 World Cup, and earlier, with what was probably the best ever German team, the 1972 European championship.

In 1975, Hennes Weisweiler was tempted to Spain as coach of CF Barcelona but he returned to the Bundesliga to take over 1st FC Köln and lead them first to the FA Cup in 1977 and a League and Cup double in 1977–78.

Most of the top coaches today prepare their players by working in squares or other restricted areas like the penalty area or half the pitch when they use a lot of players.

Every team today marks their best opponents very tightly, thus giving them no space to play in and no time to look or think.

Training in restricted areas like small squares is very much like the modern game because the lines represent opponents and if the ball passes over a line of the square it is lost. Thus the players have to develop the ability to play in very tight situations and to read the game before they get the ball.

In squares the players also learn to give their passes the correct weight because a pass that is too heavy will go over a line and be lost. Playing in restricted areas, the players can learn to develop their skill, balance and touch and read the game before they get the ball, all in very tight situations and with lines limiting their freedom of action.

Having learned to play within very tight limits in training, the game itself becomes relatively easy for good players and no one is better qualified to write about this aspect of coaching than Hennes Weisweiler who was one of the first to develop this approach to coaching.

In the way of working that I have developed, my teams play a lot of small sided games and practices in small areas. Most of them take place in a square fifteen yards by fifteen yards but for the practices involving more players, for example five against two building up to five against five, we use half of the pitch.

We play in small spaces like fifteen yard squares to learn to play in confined areas, for players have often very

little space in which to work in matches. There are
tactical reasons for playing in small squares that I will
explain later, with each different practice having its own
aims.

But at the beginning of the training session I like to
start with a practice five against two. This is designed to
improve team-work which is not so difficult against only
two opponents, but at the start of the session I use it to
bring a good spirit to the training.

Like everyone else, whatever their job, footballers do
not always feel like training. Being human, it is not possible that they all come with enthusiasm every day but I
have found that a game five against two is rather easy to
play. Certainly it is not difficult, and if anything will work
up the enthusiasm of the players.

In this five against two we start with two touches per
player, and then after a few minutes I switch to one touch.

I saw this practice, five against two, played by Brazil
during the 1970 World Cup in Mexico and we call it
"Olé". But as the Brazilians played it, the players MUST
take two touches, and we start like that because the objective in the beginning is just to keep the ball and work
up a good spirit.

After this we play five against five on half the playing
pitch and we play this with one touch or two touch and
even as in a normal game with dribbling etc. However,
we start with two touch because that is not so difficult and
switch to one touch when the players have got the feel of
things. We play one touch for seven or eight minutes, but
this practice is very, very difficult so then we switch back
to two touch and after four or five minutes we change to
normal game conditions for about seven or eight minutes.

With another seven or eight minutes for the warming-
up period of two touch, this makes a total of about
twenty minutes for this practice.

The practice two against one is designed in my way of working for two things: dribbling by the two players, and covering for the one player. I like all my players to be able to dribble because in many game situations, the man with the ball must dribble.

For the player who is alone, it is very important that he learns to jockey-off because in matches it is vital that he is not beaten. So he must learn to time his tackles and the lone defender must learn to re-position himself quickly when the two players inter-pass, changing position so that he stops the man with the ball breaking through, but also positions himself in such a way that he can also cover the second player.

In this practice we can have four or five attacking players waiting to play because we do not want the defender to be in a dribbling duel with the same player too many times. If that happened, the defender would soon learn all the attacking tricks and that would be no good for his confidence in dribbling which is vitally important.

We also change the defender quite often so that everyone gets a turn playing in defence against two men.

The game three against two also has several aims. In matches the players must work together in attack and work together in defence, so here we have two defenders working together, and three attacking players who must also work together. But in three against two, as in two against one, I like to see the man with the ball dribble past his opponent because wingers for example have to do this very often in matches.

A variation to the two against one practice is to have a goalkeeper and one defender play against one man. This practice has a direct bearing on the game because if the dribbler is successful he goes on to shoot at the goal. Again we have a group of players and the defender must play twice against each of the other players. After that we change the defender so that each player has a turn at defending and a turn at dribbling and shooting. In this practice it is more practical if the coach plays the ball to the attacking player. In this way the attacking player must stop the ball and turn before dribbling and this is more like the real game.

I can make all these small practices more difficult by instructing the attacking players that they must use only the outside, not the inside, of the foot. Amateur players may be allowed to use the inside of the foot, but for professionals it should not be too difficult to play these small practices as instructed.

Another thing I do in this one v. one and a goalkeeper practice is to make everyone play with their weaker foot. With most players the left foot is not so good, so I instruct the attacking player to use only his weaker foot both for dribbling and shooting, while the defender too can only use his weakest foot.

In the game three against one the most important thing is to try to find free space and make a penetrating run to receive a pass. With only one opponent who must offer a challenge to the man with the ball this is not too difficult. With two men close to the ball, one in possession and one in support, the third man has to try and find space. Very often the defender is cutting out the direct pass to the free man, and then of course the player with the ball has to pass back to the player in support of him and he makes the through pass for the third man.

Later in a three against two game this becomes more difficult but the players get some very good ideas about how to do this in the three against one game. One defender has to challenge the man with the ball, but the other two players are relatively free and the second defender cannot cover them both if they try to find space on either side of the man with the ball, one moving outside into what would be a wing position in the game and the other trying to go through the middle for example.

So each of the small sided practice games has got very important technical and tactical objectives.

The practices three against one and three against two, as well as four against two and five against two, are all tactical games, specially designed for teamwork in groups.

Then the practices like three against three and five against five make it more difficult for the attacking players to make things work, for in half the pitch they are training in match like conditions.

If we consider the practice three against two it is really like the game also. Here it is not possible to make the condition one touch for it is too difficult to sustain it. Dribbling and passing are combined here with the three players having all possibilities open to them.

The coach must watch the teamwork of the three players with the ball and also the combined understanding of the two defenders. Sometimes I break into the practices to say that something was very good or that something was wrong and that we must change this a little.

We also have a practice using half the pitch with five strikers playing against five defenders. There is only one goal, but otherwise it is a normal game. Here we have every possibility for combination between the left side or the right side combining with the three middle attackers. The inside player can go outside the winger, or we can play a long pass from the left side to the right side, and here, heading at goal is very important. In this practice the defenders only defend although in the game if we want to open the game from behind, then we can learn this teamwork from defence, but that is another practice. Here the defenders only defend.

In football today it is necessary to be very good with the head. But it is not possible just to run with the ball or play a long ball down the wing and then hit a high ball into the middle. We must have ideas for the attack, but we must also have ideas for keeping the ball.

In English football they lose the ball too much with long passes that are not sure. It is better to use two passes that are sure and not one pass over thirty or forty yards that is not sure. In England, maybe only ten per cent of the long passes are successful. So if we attack with two passes over middle distances, about twenty to twenty-five yards, it is more sure and we keep the ball.

When we lose the ball because a midfield player has given a long pass of about forty yards, the three or four strikers and the midfield players must all come back again. In this way all the attacking players and the midfield players lose stamina running upfield and back again.

So in the practice five strikers against five defenders we must use middle distance passes that are sure so that we do not have to give up our stamina when the ball is lost.

While all my teams have played attacking football I have never neglected to prepare the players in the defence. The game four against two is very good for this because the two defenders must work together and learn to cover each other.

All the time, one of the two defenders must attack the man in possession of the ball without being beaten, but most important, the other defender must cover the approach to goal. Above all he must position himself so that he can cut out the through pass into the free space.

If both defenders do their job properly then the only alternative open to the man with the ball is to pass square. When he makes that easy pass the two defenders must immediately change roles with the defender nearest the ball getting tight on the man then in possession while the other defender must run to take up a position where he can cover the free space and cut out any attempted through pass.

This exercise usually lasts fifteen minutes with the two defenders constantly changing. One attacks the ball and the other covers.

Four men would usually beat two quite easily so in this exercise I instruct the attacking players that they must not dribble and make it one touch only.

If the players are young and relatively inexperienced I change it to two touches which is not so difficult for them.

Working in practices like four against two and three against two is less easy for the coach who has to watch the defenders as well as the attacking players and stop the practice to explain mistakes in both phases of the game. Everything must be practical. By that I mean that it must be like the real game, so I often work with a goalkeeper added to the defenders and of course it is necessary to watch everything he does too.

At first I take only two defenders and the goalkeeper so it is not so difficult for three attacking players to combine well together. But no dribbling, only two touch, is allowed.

Then I add another attacking player and another defender to make it four against three and a goalkeeper, playing in half the pitch. At first I allow the players two touches, but with experienced first team players I can make it one touch.

If I work with three defenders and a goalkeeper against four attacking players we play normally like in a game with dribbling allowed, but they must always work in the direction of the goal, and not just keep possession. When a player dribbles he cuts out one of the defenders as in a real game and they must press the attack quickly. I think that is very important. In real games there are many opportunities to counter-attack and then we must speed up the game and play fast. Fast, but not too fast for we must always try to be sure with our passes. As I have already stated it is better to play two middle distance passes than one pass over fifty yards that is not sure.

In the practice four against two and a goalkeeper I want the players to play with two touches only to improve their combination play. But later if I add a *libero* or sweeper as it is in England, then it is like a real game and then I encourage the players to dribble and go up alone.

So after the first few minutes of five against two to get everyone into the right mood I often begin with the practice three against one. Then I allow only two touches. But after a few minutes I bring in another defender and soon build it up to three against three, with the attacking three all strikers. Then everything is allowed including dribbling and one-twos etc.

In all the practices two things are very important. The attacking players must have good ideas and good habits. They must also run in support of each other.

I also work with the defensive players so that they come out in support when we get the ball. I think the players like this too when they can go upfield. Because the defensive players practise as attacking players in the small sided games as well as players who play in midfield or are strikers, they can play very well.

This is important because it does not seem to be hard work for the players to run a lot if they are playing with the ball. Straightforward running without a ball seems like hard work, but when they take part in practices, say five against five, it is pleasure as well as work.

I like all my defenders to be able to go upfield and I give them all the opportunity to practise in attacking positions in the small sided games. I would not have a defender who can only defend.

In the game there is a constant change between defence

and attack and all the back four players should be involved. I want my centre backs to go up too.

In England only one or two players from the defence get involved in the attacks of their teams. The right backs and the left backs go upfield but English centre backs very rarely move up. In my team all players must be working for defence and attack, even the centre backs.

In the game the forwards must go back to help the defence so that we defend with eleven men in our own half. Then we attack with five or six players. Two wingers are very important for modern attacking football and therefore I play with two wingers and one centre forward, not with two spearheads in the centre.

Although I want every player to be involved with both defence and attack, it is very important to my way of thinking that each player should be specially good at one aspect of the game.

I do not like the kind of midfield player who works hard but cannot go up and shoot. Neither do I like a midfield player who is not strong in defence. One or maybe two midfield players must specialise in covering in defence or man to man markings, as well as working in midfield.

Very many midfield players can run all day between one penalty area and the other but they are not specially good at anything in the game.

Similarly, although I want my centre forward to be a strong attacking player who gets goals regularly, I also want him to be able to challenge an opponent or cover a midfield player. So he must have a little bit of experience in defence. Such a centre forward can gain this experience by playing as a defender in small sided games, and the coach must be able to see what he does not understand or cannot do, and help him to overcome all his difficulties.

On the other hand, the right back and the left back must

have speed, strength and determination to challenge and fight against their wingers but they must also have the ability to go forward and cross the ball well. So in two v. one games the full backs, as well as the wingers, have to develop the skills to dribble to get into good positions for crossing the ball, just like the wingers. So in the two v. one games, all the players learn how to attack and how to defend.

We practise this way because I like to have in my team, specialists who can also do other things well.

Some midfield players also have the ability to be good defenders so they drop back to cover for back four players who go upfield. But usually the most gifted attacking midfield players do not have this ability. A good midfield player who is the director of the attack would be wasted in defence.

I like specialists who can help out in more ways than one and I try to get the players to play to their strengths and within their limitations. So if a back four player attacks, I arrange for a midfield player to cover him, but never the director of the attack who will probably be quite good at scoring goals as well as organising the midfield, and who would be wasted at the back. I let players do what they do best.

Playing with two wingers my teams score quite a lot of goals from crosses. But if they are to be successful they must be the right kind of crosses. The English make a big mistake here, putting over high crosses into the penalty area from any angle, and from various distances. In England the ball can be crossed by a winger, the full back or a midfield player, but they do it from too far out from the goal line.

We try to get behind the defence to the goal line before crossing the ball. Maybe the winger and the full back up in support combine, or the winger has to dribble and beat a man to get there, and then we play the cross ball from the goal line.

The advantages are that the ball comes from behind the defenders. In this situation the defenders have problems and all the advantages go to the attacking team.

We work at this in the practice five against five using half the pitch. If the winger has the ball and is being challenged by the full back he cannot just cross the ball. In the middle are the centre forward and two defenders, the centre back marking him and the *libero*. I say the winger MUST DRIBBLE because he cannot pass to the centre forward when he is marked by two men. The same would apply if it was an attacking full back who had the ball, for they must beat the defender in a one v. one duel before crossing the ball. I always say that if a good winger in this situation does not dribble then he is not in good form.

In training I order that the man with the ball must dribble in this situation, because if he gets past the full back the *libero* must come to challenge him, and that leaves the centre forward with only one man to beat.

When the player with the ball gets to the goal line he can choose between crossing the ball, and passing the ball back which is sometimes better for the striker and the midfield players up in support. Passes pulled back are for the midfield players to shoot. In this situation the midfield players are coming from the blind side of the defenders who must turn to face the ball. During matches, the players must decide what to do, whether to cross the ball or pull it back from the goal line.

It is the same in midfield. Sometimes the player with the ball gives a pass to one of the strikers and sometimes he decides to run with the ball.

There is no special preparation or other practices before we play these small sided games. All I want is good players, and we work together in the small sided games. Only then can I influence the players.

In the game two against one when a winger has the ball I can insist that he beats the defender before passing, and I can always stop the practice and tell the players what I want them to do next time.

For example, in the exercise five defenders v. five strikers I might stop the game and say that was OK, or that was not good. Then I tell the players how we must change our way of playing a little.

Sometimes the players make a mistake in changing positions in front of the ball. A player gives the ball to the left winger and then goes inside looking for a return pass. I can point out that it is better not to make a run in front of the opponents, but to go looking for a pass by running behind the opponent—on his blind side. An opponent is surprised by a pass to a man who has gone on his blind side, and the pass is effective. So I stop the exercise and talk about it.

If we have a player near the penalty area who gives the ball to the winger and then stays in support, thinking the winger might want to return the pass, then I stop the practice. This happens very often. In this situation, I want the man who gives the pass to sprint immediately to the near post, looking for the cross. All our attacks will be more successful if we have the centre forward looking for the long cross at the far post, and the player who put the winger away, looking for the short cross to the near post.

When this crops up in the practice five v. five, I stop them and tell the players so that they know for the games, what I want to see from them. All the two v. one and three v. two games are mostly free, but even then I stop them if I see something that is not good. Maybe I have to inform the player with the ball that he is not screening it from his opponent. It is small things like that which it is necessary for the coach to see. Younger coaches possibly do not see these little things, and others overlook them because perhaps they think they are not so important.

I like very much to work with good young players, to get them to work at the game and give them my ideas. Maybe with young players it is best to let them work in all the exercises with two touches at first because it is not so difficult.

The most important things for new young players are skill, and later speed. Then the coach must work with the player and teach him everything he knows. Intelligence for the game is also very important so that when I explain something, or show him something, he can understand and change his way of playing to do this thing the way I want it. Even the very small things. Confidence is also very important. A young player lacking in confidence would have problems trying to improve. But the coach must work with the young players and talk to them.

To work with young players is very satisfying and I demonstrate things to them. It is important to inform them exactly, very precisely about skills. For example, to cross the ball into the goalmouth it is very important to play the ball with the instep and I must explain exactly and demonstrate.

Sometimes the young player stands too near the ball when in possession. The position of the ball in relation to the player is very important for all skills, and I look for such small things with new young players.

Many young players coming up into the first team squad as professionals have not developed the full range of skills to a high enough degree. So I work with them on skills very often, and they improve. It is also very satisfying and very rewarding to work with good young players. Soon after I joined 1st FC Köln in 1977 we won the German FA Cup largely through our young right back. He learned to cross the ball correctly very quickly, and moving upfield very often, he laid on the crosses for our centre forward Dieter Müller to score two goals.

To work in restricted areas like the small sided games in fifteen yard squares, the players must have good habits. I give them these good habits, but it is also necessary for the players to make decisions. I help them to make good decisions by coaching them in squares and explaining everything.

My old team Mönchengladbach was always a team with very good attacking ideas and now with Köln it is the same. That is my system, my ideas based on attacking football, and we score more goals than anyone else.

So any coach can take these ideas and get the players to play two v. one or four v. two, but it is necessary to have experience to see the good things and to pick up the faults.

To be a good coach it is necessary to have a talent for it, as in all walks of life. Talent, experience and working. And it is necessary always to be busy with football.

If I can offer some advice to young coaches who will read this book, do everything in squares. Instruct the players only to use the left foot or the right foot, paying particular attention to the weak foot of each player, and vary this by insisting that all players use the instep only or the outside of the foot only.

We work each day for heading too. I know English players have strength in heading, so we must improve. Every training day we work at high crosses—the instep cross, from the right and from the left, with four players in front of goal. The players who cross the ball must have excellent skills with the outside of the foot. We work at the low ground cross from close in and also for the high ball and the medium height ball.

All coaches have problems and the only answer is to

work at them. My way of thinking and working, my specialist style, is attacking football. I cannot let my players concentrate on defence when we are leading 1–0. I bring up young players to play attacking football and if I am successful it is because I encourage young players to work at the game, to think about the game as I do, wanting to score a goal every time they get possession of the ball.

3/ The Direct and Indirect Styles

Dave Sexton was born in London on 6th April 1930. As a player he was an inside forward with Luton Town, West Ham, Leyton Orient, Brighton and Crystal Palace, and played for an FA Representative XI.

After retiring from the active side of the game he became the Chelsea coach in 1961 and remained there until he became manager of Leyton Orient for the 1965–66 season. Then followed six months as coach of Fulham and eighteen months as coach of Arsenal between 1966 and 1967, when he became manager-coach of Chelsea in the 1967–68 season.

Eight seasons at Chelsea were climaxed by winning the FA Cup in 1970 and the European Cupwinners Cup in 1971 when Chelsea beat Real Madrid 2–1 after a 1–1 draw and extra time in Athens.

In 1974 Dave Sexton left Chelsea to become manager-coach of Queen's Park Rangers where he remained until he became manager-coach of Manchester United in 1977–78 season. With Queen's Park Rangers he proved that good football and success are not incompatible, and early in 1978 he was appointed manager of the England Under 21 team.

In 1977, Dave Sexton was invited to Holland by the Dutch FA to lecture and give practical demonstrations of what he thought were the basic differences between the British game and that generally played on the European mainland.

Later in the year he was invited to stage practical coaching demonstrations along similar lines at the UEFA Coaches Conference and much of this chapter is on the same themes.

But giving this contribution a novel twist, Dave Sexton reveals a theme on which he has recently been doing a lot of work, coaching British players to run at the opponents with the ball at their feet, rather than play the ball forward. This he believes is the first step towards good football because so many good things can come out of it.

In general terms the British way of playing football is very direct and using a military analogy, this approach leads directly to a face to face confrontation as in the First World War between 1914 and 1918. In that war there were a great many men killed and wounded because it was a face to face confrontation with neither side prepared to give way. This direct approach obviously led to a great waste of many lives.

Another way of waging war is a bit more subtle. As the Chinese say "make progress in the way that water makes progress. If water comes up against an obstacle it is very patient, and it persists. Water will find a way around an obstacle, or find a crack that it can go through".

This is an indirect approach.

I would say that this sums up quite basically, the direct British approach, and the more indirect approach of the continental Europeans. The British game is based to a great extent on the direct approach whereas the best of the continental Europeans are more indirect.

It is very interesting to consider the offshoots of the two basically different approaches to soccer:

1. the British have very many brave players
2. the British are very good at heading

3. the continental players have had to improve their passing

4. the continentals are more subtle

In Britain we still tend to attack in straight lines with our direct approach. We go straight down the middle with one long pass or we go straight down this side of the field or that, and then put the ball straight across into the middle.

Other countries that have adopted the more indirect approach have had to develop more movement off the ball—intelligent movement. So on the continent you can see a lot of players rotating in the area around the ball, and a lot of cross-running by players in pairs.

Clearly, if a coach decides that his players have not got the power for the direct approach, then he has to start thinking and develop other ideas. But in Britain, where we have powerful players, we have tended to play to them and not bother to think of anything else.

Not having powerful players, the continentals have been forced to think about other things. But now there is an urge to seek common ground.

FC Bayern Munich and Ajax both wanted to obtain the transfer of the Scottish international centre forward, Joe Jordan. Obviously they wanted, at least, to have another option in their attacking plans.

In Britain we have been left behind in terms of movement off the ball, but we should be able to develop what are now, largely continental European ideas. We could do this quite easily, and combined with our power, such a situation would do the British game a great deal of good.

Combined with the inherent qualities of English players, this intelligent movement off the ball would, I am sure, make England really strong again in the football world.

If a British team is doing well—if your centre forward

is beating the opposing centre back in the air, and if your wingers are beating their full backs and getting the ball across, then you can succeed by attacking in straight lines.

But if you find that your centre forward is being beaten in the air and you are not scoring goals by using a direct approach, it would be very useful to be able to change your style of play in the middle of a match and adopt a less direct approach.

The most important thing is to convince the players that more movement off the ball will be useful. In my experience, players will take to anything if they believe it will make them better players and will bring better results.

On the other hand, young players are easy to mould and coaches could start them off immediately playing a more universal game. But established British players would first have to be persuaded that it will add to their game and be useful.

Having described the two schools of football, the two basic philosophies, we can now take practical examples to illustrate the direct and indirect approaches.

The direct approach is by and large an aerial approach to goal, most pronounced in the final third of the pitch. Not all the time, but most of the time, British teams get the ball to a wide position in the last third of the pitch and then the ball goes over, high to the far post.

The indirect approach shows up most in the final third of the pitch for when the continentals get the ball to a wide position, the ball does not go over into the goal-mouth, for they invariably try something different. There are several points to be made about the aerial approach. First, from the viewpoint of the defending goalkeeper the high cross is very worrying. It is a useful tool, not to be dismissed.

However, you can still tidy things up. The centre forward for example, tends to go for the far post with his marker in attendance. Forwards tend to allow defenders to get too close to them, in positions where a nudge or a little touch at the right moment can easily put a forward off balance. This often prevents forwards getting in clear headers at goal.

To edge forward towards goal is an instinctive thing.

Forwards who get into this position should be coached to pull away from the man marking them, immediately before the ball is crossed. If they make backward space as described in Diagram 4, pulling away from their mar-

Diagram 4

ker, then as the ball comes over, the forward can go to meet the ball and take off on the run, jumping higher with a single foot take-off.

If the ball overshoots the far post area and the forward has made backward space as indicated then he has space in which to take the ball on his chest and shoot, or alternatively he can nod the ball back across the goal-mouth for a colleague.

Players tend naturally to press in towards goal, but I would like to see them make space backwards before the ball comes in, and then go in violently and quickly, so that they are composed when they meet the ball.

That solves the problem of the crowded penalty area. Players should try to get in by all means, but if they find they are tightly marked, they should pull away, as in Diagram 4, with all the advantages described.

From observation of games you will see that very often the ball flies over the heads of everyone in the goalmouth. But by pulling away as described, they can still make use of these crosses.

If the defender goes with the spearhead as he pulls away, this creates space for a midfield player to make a run and have the chance to get in a header at goal, as described in Diagram 5.

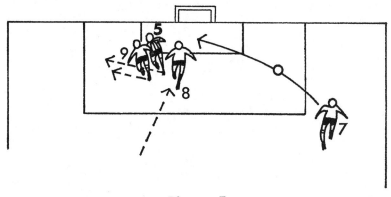

Diagram 5

To practice this I start with just three players, one to cross, and the forward and his marker. All I want is to see the forward pull away backwards and then depending on the cross, sprint forward and jump to head at goal, or take the ball on his chest and shoot.

After a few minutes I add two midfield players, 4 and 8 in Diagram 6. The midfield player 4 passes to the right back 2 who is out wide, while player 8 takes every chance to sprint forward to get in a header at goal when he sees that the defender 5 has followed the striker 9 as he made space backwards.

Now I built up the practice by bringing in more players,

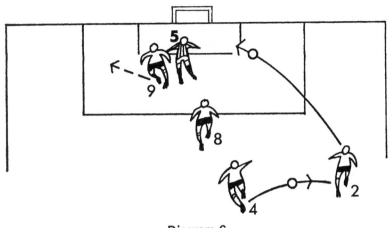

Diagram 6

3, 10 and another striker 7 who will be marked by defender 3 and will face crosses coming in from the left flank,
as described in Diagram 7. Diagram 8 shows the two
attacks, working in turn one after the other, with the
emphasis on the spearheads to pull back and make space
in front of them so that they can go forward to head at
goal, or alternatively take the ball on the chest and shoot.

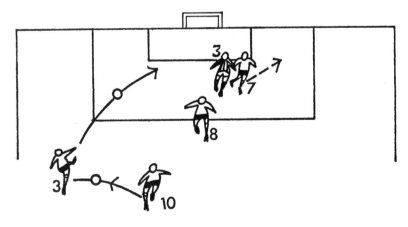

Diagram 7

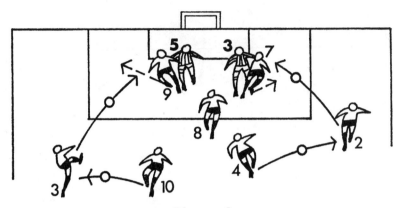

Diagram 8

To add variety to the types of crosses I now ask the midfield players to cross the ball, in turn, as described for the two flanks in Diagram 9. First the midfield player lays the ball up to the striker not involved in that cross, receives the ball back and crosses to the far post area as indicated.

All the time we are looking for the striker to pull back out of the goalmouth and for the midfield player 8 to nip in and get in a header if the defender follows the striker as he pulls away backwards.

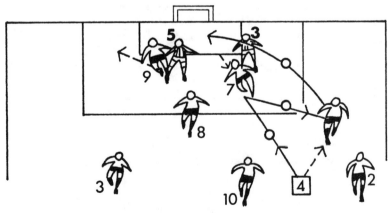

Diagram 9

The strikers have to work very hard at it for the natural tendency is to press in on goal, and stay there to "fight" for the cross.

Finally I introduce a variation in that the wide player can now choose whether to knock the ball over the back to the spearhead at the far post, or he can try to curl little balls in to the near post area for the midfield player 8 to dive in and score with a header at the near post. So we have a variety of crosses.

When the central strikers begin to pull away backwards you will begin to see players being able to use their chest and volley their shots at goal which is a thing of grace and class in the penalty area.

But as already pointed out this cannot be done if the striker is pinned up against a man marking him.

Cyrille Regis of West Bromwich Albion scored a fine goal in the 1977–78 season. Regis is at the far post with the centre back running backwards trying to get a header in, but failing, and Regis takes the ball on his chest and scores with a good shot.

It is the positioning of Regis that makes it all possible. But there is also the skill with which he controls the ball on his chest—and the shot. But it was his positioning that was critical, for if he had not been in the right place he would not have had the chance to use his skills.

So there are quite a lot of coaching points to be made with regard to crosses and the players must work hard at them in training.

For an example of the indirect approach I took something I had seen when, as manager of Chelsea, we had played Feyenoord in Rotterdam. The Dutch side played very well in that match and beat us 3–1.

Right at the start we were doing so badly that I had to look very carefully to see what was going wrong.

All the Chelsea players, practically our whole team

seemed to be in our own penalty area. We could not get out of our penalty area, and Feyenoord were smashing in shots all over the place.

Any number of Feyenoord players seemed to be having free shots from the edge of our penalty area, and they were doing it by getting the ball to wide positions from which British players would usually knock in the high ball. Feyenoord were not knocking the ball over however, but were doing a very simple thing that was causing total confusion within the Chelsea team. After the match the Feyenoord coach told me that in the season just ended, his team had earned 18 penalty kicks and scored from 17 of them as a result of the simple thing they were doing, which is described in Diagram 10.

They had two centre forwards pressing in towards goal (8 and 9) with the ball out wide in possession of the winger. But he did not cross it. The ball was played back to the supporting full back who played it on to the nearest midfield player on that side. Now came the critical part, for the centre forward 8, with the ball coming from the left wing, now sprinted back to the edge of the penalty

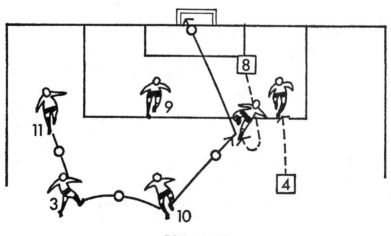

Diagram 10

area, while the midfield player 4 dived into the box, ostensibly looking for a header. This worked like magic, for the left sided midfield player now had a free man to pass to, player 8, and he could get in a shot, as in the Diagram.

It worked so well because the Chelsea centre backs would not follow their man, but maintained their position to clear the cross. In addition the Chelsea player marking the midfield man who dived into the penalty area, quite rightly followed his man, for no good midfield player will allow the man he is marking to get into the penalty area unopposed.

Thus we repeatedly found that we had two men close to goal marking a midfield player while the centre forward was unmarked and shooting from the edge of the penalty area.

Feyenoord did this from both the left wing and the right wing, with players 9 and 10 making the switch when the ball was out wide on the right.

To practise this it is best done without opposition, disposing the eight players needed according to Diagram 11. With the ball on the right it goes back to 2 and in to 4,

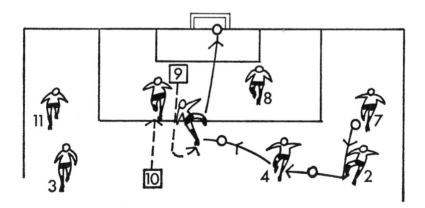

Diagram 11

while 9 and 10 switch positions. Then 4 gives 9 a good pass with which he can shoot.

Now try it on the left with players 11, 3 and 10 taking part in the build-up, while players 8 and 4 do the switch. Player 10 passes to 8 and he looks up and shoots at goal.

In that Chelsea–Feyenoord game, the Dutch were successful with an indirect approach because the central defenders naturally would not come out and the Chelsea midfield players followed the men they were marking. Thus Chelsea repeatedly found themselves with two men marking one in the goalmouth, while Feyenoord had created a shooting space on the edge of the Chelsea penalty area.

This highlighted to me the basic difference in approach between Chelsea and Feyenoord at that time. Chelsea would get the ball to a wide position and put it in high while Feyenoord would get the ball out wide and try to out-manouvre their opponents.

The principle on which Feyenoord played was based on a chess like approach: how are we going to make a shooting space close to goal?

So we can sum up:

In the direct approach we just leave the defenders there and battle for the high ball

In the indirect approach, the attacking team tries to winkle defenders out somehow.

I do not know whether this little switch was copied from basketball or vice versa, but it is definitely a move from basketball which is a very sophisticated game.

In my opinion basketball is a microcosm of all the problems in football. Basketball has had some very good minds thinking about their game for many years, and is now very highly developed. They have developed techniques for blocking people out and for screening too.

But the most interesting point about basketball is that they have two basic ways to attack:

One is to have a "fast break" following the opponent having an unsuccessful attempt at your basket. In this you gain possession in defence and get the ball down the other end as fast as you can before the enemy can get back; the other way to attack is to go into what they call a "pattern offence". In pattern offences they do not go for speed, which allows their opponents to re-group, but they run their "pattern" which is designed to make a hole in the enemy defence which will allow someone to get in and score.

This sophisticated approach to basketball is what has interested me in the game. Frequently while playing against continental teams, I have noted one basic "pattern play" played against my team, although it can have slight variations.

In Diagram 12 this "pattern" is described. The wingers will suddenly sprint into the middle, and simultaneously the centre forward will move out and drop back. Then the midfield men make runs wide on the flanks.

What the attacking team does then will depend on how the opposition reacts. If their defenders follow the men they are marking, then the attacking team will utilise the space they have left; if they do not follow their individual opponents then the runners get free to receive a pass.

This is a typical example of what Franz Beckenbauer used to do all the time when he was playing in Germany.

If the right back in Diagram 12 follows the left winger he leaves space that player 10 can exploit. But if the full back stays in position then the left winger is running free, and the sweeper has to pick him up, so he isn't sweeping any more!

So a simple little "pattern play" can pull defenders all over the place.

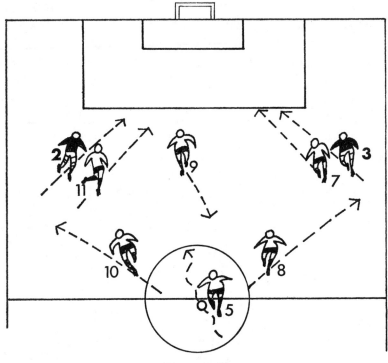

Diagram 12

You can see this type of play in many continental European countries although I am not sure where it originated. Perhaps it was in Yugoslavia, where they are very good thinkers about the game.

So this indirect approach is an alternative to attacking in straight lines, and I feel that if we can get a bit of that approach into our game in Britain it will be a big help.

The interesting point that came out of my coaching trip to Holland was that the Dutch coaches told me that their fans liked English football because they find it exciting. It is exciting, because every time we cross the ball in the air, it is up for grabs.

But the indirect approach is a much more studious one and the crime with them is giving the ball away.

In Britain we are not worried about losing the ball and stick it into the penalty area. That of course increases the tempo and leads to more incidents. Dutch fans apparently yearn for a bit of excitement while I think the British game would benefit if we thought about it a little more, and get our players to vary their approach sometimes.

It can be done because the nice thing about Holland in the 1974 World Cup was that they were very well organised and very talented as an attacking force, but they were also very good at getting the ball back as well. Rinus Michels explains in his contribution to this book how he organised that.

Playing against a number of good teams on the continent of Europe, and especially Borussia Mönchengladbach I have been struck by one thing that could be very important for English football, and the game everywhere.

When we get the ball in Britain, there is a tendency to pass the ball forward or sideways. But watching Mönchengladbach, I have seen that whenever anyone got the ball, he ran forward with it.

Mönchengladbach are the best example, because no matter which player got the ball he went forward with it at his feet. It seems to me that this is the essence of good football—the spring that all the good moves come from. Passing the ball forward does not have the same effect, does not produce the good moves. So if you want this response from your players it will have to be worked on in training.

What follows when a player goes forward with the ball at his feet are two things:

1. If there is space in front of him, the player with the ball goes on running forward with the ball unchallenged

2. If the player with the ball is challenged by an opponent, which he will be sooner or later, he can do one

of two things. He can dribble past the man or he can use a one-two with a colleague to play his way past the challenger.

If the player that offers a challenge has had to leave the man he was marking then immediately the player with the ball has a free colleague to pass to and get the return ball in space.

Alternatively, if the man with the ball looks at the free man and feints to pass, this will help him to dribble past the challenger, for the chances are that he will buy the feint.

Of course there is a lot involved here. The coach must work on the type and quality of the pass that goes "in" to the free man. He must also work on the pass that comes back. Then there is the ability of the man with the ball to beat his challenger and go forward. So there is a lot of good technique involved.

But it seemed to me, watching Borussia Mönchengladbach that this is the spring, the essence of good football because when you work at it, so many good things come out of it.

Naturally, you will not get the responses you want from your players unless you work at it in training.

When you try it you will find that it is quite hard work. With this response from your players, the game becomes very demanding physically because there is an urgency about it. But on the other hand, when it is done well in a game it is very economic.

When I first thought about this theme, I remembered what Arthur Rowe, the former Tottenham Hotspur manager, once said to me about being unable to understand that people only start to think of one-twos when they get outside the opponent's penalty area.

It is clear that players should think about one-twos when they first get the ball, even deep in their own half.

With good one-twos you can cut through the attack and the midfield of your opponent . . . like a knife through butter.

There are many things that will come out of coaching players to run forward with the ball. First of all, the players must get out of the habit of letting the opponent get too close before passing the ball. If the opponent is close enough, he has only to stretch a leg quickly to deflect the ball or even nick it. So that is the first point to watch for.

If you tell the players to try it in a game say seven v. five, the coach should repeatedly tell the players in good time "do it early". In fact, the pass should be made almost as soon as the marker comes off the man he is leaving free.

With the ball on the way to the free man, and the player who made the pass sprinting into space (if he can find it), the player now receiving the ball has first of all to decide if the return pass is "on".

Laying off the ball first time is very important. The quality of the ball played back to the runner is vital.

But the player receiving the first pass might see someone moving to intercept the return pass!

This will be more likely if the player receiving the first pass turns his body sideways-on to the approaching ball. Now he will not only be able to see a possible interception but, assuming he has space behind him, he now has the alternative to let the ball run, and follow it himself.

Now there is a vital point here, which again is highlighted in basketball.

A man marked by an opponent on his left will hold out his right arm when he wants the ball. This will tell his colleague in possession, exactly where he wants the ball put.

In football we have the same situation. If a marked

player is to be able to play the ball, it must always be given to his back foot because then he can play the ball while screening it from his opponent.

If the player receiving the one-two elects not to give the ball back, he now has to turn to run with the ball towards goal himself. Meanwhile, all the other players have to make a new decision according to the changed circumstances and re-position themselves accordingly.

If you multiply this running with the ball towards goal by all the players in the team, and what can come out of it, you are playing good football, for we are also asking players to develop the skill to dribble past opponents.

So starting from this simple little thing we can get an awful lot out of it and it becomes very important for the game as a whole.

If you try it, starting with two against one and building it up, adding players, and always giving them a goal to aim for, you will find that a lot of players will prefer to play what I call comfortable football. This is easy paced stuff with a minimum of effort. For example, first time square passes or back passes. But for the good of the game we want to see attacking football so we must coach the players to turn on the ball and go forward with it.

Some players do this quite naturally, but many others do not. If we can introduce this aspect of the game into football it will help the game a lot because so many good things come out of it.

Once a player is propelled forward he has now got to start making decisions. Shall he hold it or play it off? But now you are playing good football.

When you coach this aspect of the game, work at the little things involved to make it more certain that your side will retain the ball and get through.

Work at things like letting the ball go early—before the opponent is close enough to intercept the pass; work at the angle of the pass given, and the player who receives the ball deciding whether to give it back or not.

Before leaving this theme I would like to say that it is not my own creation, for the idea came to me while watching Borussia Mönchengladbach. But the perceptive coach will always be looking for new ideas, from his own team, from opponents, and from anyone else he happens to see. One can even get good ideas from watching other ball games for I am convinced that they all have a lot in common.

For example, I once happened to pick up a book on rugby, written by Ray Williams who is Director of Coaching for the Rugby Association of Wales. He set out his basic principles for good rugby:

1. Go forward
2. Support the man with the ball
3. When forward movement is halted, change the direction of attack
4. When you lose possession, apply pressure to get it back.

Clearly all ball games have a lot in common. Basketball rugby, soccer. Go forward, support, re-direct attack. It all has a familiar ring to a football coach.

But it all starts with one man going forward with the ball.

4/ The "Block System" Based on Counter Attacking

by **Vaclav Jezek**

Vaclav Jezek was born at Zvolen, a small town in Slovakia near Banska Bystrica on 1st October 1923. He began playing as an attacking centre half and then as the tactics changed through WM to 4–2–4, switched to right half and right midfield.

Between 1946 and 1950 he played for the Czech First Division club SK Hradec Kralove, earning Provincial representative honours, and from 1950 to 1955 played for Slavia Liberec.

With Slavia Liberec he began coaching, while still playing, training the club's Under 18 team. From there he took over Division Two side Jiskra Liberec and after a spell with Lokomotiva Ceska Lipa, moved to Prague in 1960 to become coach of the Youth team of Dukla Prague.

In 1963 he became coach of Sparta Prague, leading them to two championships and one FA Cup win, and in July 1969, went to Holland to look after FC Den Haag for three seasons.

Returning to Prague in June 1972, he took over the Czech national team and, rebuilding the side, eventually led them to success in the final of the 1976 European Championship.

Czechoslovakia were one of the traditional Central European giants of soccer with the feats of Jozef Bican almost legend. But since 1962 when the Czechs reached the World Cup Final and scored first against Brazil through Jozef Masopust, they have fallen behind other countries.

This is entirely due to the fact that at club level they still play the slow, short-passing game known as the Céske Ulicka, literally translated as "street football".

Even the generation of Masopust, Ladislav Novak and Svatopluk Pluskal who did so well in 1962 were short passing experts and Masopust's final goal was tapped in from close range.

Another problem revolves around the more physical approach to soccer adopted in recent years, for the Czechs of the necessary character usually take up ice hockey, at which the Czechs are often European and World champions. Those who play soccer are usually those who still look upon the game as an art, and it shows in their domestic game which is still slow and skilful.

It was against this background, knowing he had to adapt the Czechs' natural style of play, that Vaclav Jezek had to work in order to win the 1976 European Championship.

Playing to a counter-attacking system, the attacks begin in the moment that one of our players gains possession of the ball. Then we can look at the development of an attack in three phases:

1. To switch the team from a defensive posture into an attacking one
2. To develop the attack and carry it forward into our opponent's half of the field
3. The final phase—pressing the attack to a shot or header at the enemy goal.

Speed is vital in the first and third phases, though no time should be wasted in the second stage. In phase one, the ball should be played forward very quickly in order to cut opponents out of the game for this makes it impossible for them to get back and reinforce their defence.

Then in the final stage, pressing the attack on goal and finishing with a goalscoring attempt should also be executed at the maximum possible speed, though in stage two, as the attack develops, speed may be regarded as less important than accuracy of passing as long as there are not too many time-wasting back passes to supporting colleagues.

Although speed is of the essence in counter-attacking it can be complicated by many factors, not least the positioning of our defenders and midfield players who may be so deep that they need time to get out and take up attacking and supporting positions.

Thus our attacking trio may often have to press an attack without support and therefore every practice in the final assault on goal should be with only three players against four defenders and a goalkeeper, because no matter how they play, most of our opponents attempt to keep their defence intact and very well organised.

It has been stated that in general terms there should not be too many time-wasting back passes, but the strikers should be instructed that unless they see a very good opportunity to break through to a shooting position or create a goal chance for a colleague, they should not turn away from their supporting colleagues but should play the ball back to one of them. This helps to keep the attacking unit compact and prevents the strikers isolating themselves from support.

Thus the intelligence of the players is very important because while we want to press our attacks very quickly but stay compact as much as possible we do not want to waste time on useless or unnecessary passing.

In our earliest training sessions it became clear that while we want to build up our attacks quickly without running the risk of losing the ball through bad passing, many of the players were more concerned about safety than speed. This had to be put right but it was a problem because it was in conflict with the natural way of playing the players had developed in Czech League football where the build up is slow and accurate.

On the other hand, however, after a little encouragement our full backs and *libero* began quite quickly to reinforce the midfield players and even join in the final assault on goal. Thus our attacking play became more equally divided among all the players in the team.

At the same time however it became clear that as the tempo of our build-up in attack developed, too many promising situations broke down because the quality of the passing at top speed was not good.

This improved after special practices aimed at improving first-time passing but as it improved, the element of surprise disappeared from our play. But if our attacks therefore became more predictable, the full backs and midfield players began to combine very well on the flanks with our wingers, even in pressing to the final assault on goal.

Looking at our situation objectively, we recognised that we had no big personalities around whom we could build our team. Only goalkeeper Ivo Viktor was outstanding amongst our players.

In addition, our players do not generally have physical fitness and stamina comparable with the British and West German professionals, and neither did they tackle with the power and zeal of the players in most other countries.

Finally, while the modern international game highlights at least the occasional long pass, Czech players still tend to keep the ball close and their passes short—along traditional lines.

Summing up our situation, we knew that we could not

improve all these features of the game in a short time. To do that might require one whole football generation, or more.

For this reason we looked at our squad of representative players for specific possibilities in the field of tactics. We wanted to design a style of play that could be quickly understood by the players and successfully performed.

We emphasised to our players that in creating attacking opportunities and pressing them to goal, the defensive players immediately behind the point of attack must move forward in support. It followed that the other defenders and midfield players who were temporarily in our defensive zone also had to move forward quickly—to the halfway line—for two essential reasons:

1. By moving forward the defence removes the danger away from our goal because the operative offside line is now moved to the halfway line. Any members of the opposing side who do not react as quickly as our defenders cannot therefore take part in a quick counter-attack that might develop if we should lose the ball.

2. By moving the defence upfield as "a block", we prevented the creation of a gap between defence and attack, and the team stayed compact, as one unit. Being in relatively close support of the attacking players, everyone in the defensive block was therefore nicely placed to go forward and join in the attack, as and when the opportunities arose.

The midfield players performed a vital role in this switch from defence to attack. Not only did an attack in strength depend on them breaking out quickly into attacking positions, but they also provided the key to gaining local numerical advantage in the area around the ball.

In this way the midfield players were able to play an important role in our attacking play, which was above all based on combined play between the entire team, regardless of position.

Thus our attacking play was based above all on combined play for we lacked the outstanding individuals in attack that characterised football in former days, like many other teams.

Attacking by combined play is currently typical of all the Central European teams, many of whom have produced excellent performances and very good results. But if we lacked the big personalities that once dominated the play, it was essential that the majority of our players had a very high degree of skill in passing under pressure, were generally skilled in an all-round sense, and had a very good idea of our tactical intentions. They also required the necessary physical condition to permit them to play a full role in both defence and attack.

To make our style of play successful it was essential that the individual players were creatively active in the sense that they frequently changed position, as against the orthodox play of wingers and a centre forward who maintain their general positions all the time. Above all they had to be of the kind who were happy with the ball and not likely to give it away under pressure—players that were able to look around, with and without the ball, and take up new positions at every stage as the attacks developed. This style of play produced a lot of variety, producing all kinds of passes, both short and long, as well as the ability to beat an opponent and, very important, the ability to give the kind of pass that could be easily received and automatically "screened" from opponents. This last required a lot of work in training.

Speed in mounting and pressing attacks was vital if we were to be successful in our chosen style of play. So it follows that the number of passes had to be kept to an absolute minimum, according to the situation. Therefore the players had to think in terms of keeping the game simple and direct. Straight to goal by the quickest possible means, was the key. Any unnecessary passing simply gave our opponents more time to reinforce their defence and thus give them a better chance of stifling our attacks.

But at first our build-up in attack was too slow. With every pass came the risk that the ball would be intercepted and so we tried to simplify our attacking moves, cut out over elaborate play and become more direct.

One of the characteristics of the game we developed was that we used the spaces on the flanks more, and emphasised combined play on the wings. We chose to concentrate attacks on the flanks, partly because these were usually covered by only one opponent, the full back, and because by encouraging our own full backs and midfield players to utilise space on the flanks we were able to outnumber our opponents in these areas.

Using the space near the sidelines we were able to stretch our opponent's defence and create larger spaces elsewhere within their defensive zone which we could exploit because the gaps between the defenders that had to be covered, had been enlarged.

Obviously, if we could concentrate two or three players around the ball on the flanks, it was easier to penetrate the opposing defence. We did this most by going around the line of defenders rather than trying to go through it. Clearly, however, it would have been wrong to insist that our attacking players should never try to penetrate the enemy defence on their own. But in general it can be said that only our right winger Marian Masny had the ability and speed to create a breakthrough on his own.

Direct penetration was the hallmark of the old "third back" game of WM, when the wingers and centre forward sought to receive a long pass delivered from their own half, dropped beyond the line of defenders, for the forwards to chase and hopefully, break through to goal.

With most teams today playing with a covering player behind their defence, such passes can very rarely be exploited, but this does not mean that there are not times when a well placed individual, receiving the ball before the enemy can reinforce their defence, cannot break through on his own. Masny was often successful in such actions, and he moved from the right wing to the left, seeking such chances, and was encouraged to try and go through alone to make the initial break.

One of the prerequisites for success in such individual actions is that the attacking player should be faster than his opponents. Therefore, when Masny found that he could not out-sprint his enemies, he looked around for supporting players, and joined in an attack by combined play.

There are advantages in combined play in all three phases of an attack that cannot be stressed too highly:

Winning the ball in defence, an accurate pass forward cuts out any number of enemy players who have pressed forward. Providing our attack is pressed quickly, they will have no chance to get back into the game.

In developing the attack, dribbling is not excluded, but the comparatively wide open spaces in midfield make good "safe" passing easier.

Pressing the attack to a shot on goal is easier if the ball is passed to a colleague who makes a first-time effort, for the man in possession in and around the penalty area is the focus of attention for all the defenders, while colleagues are better able to try an attempt on goal if they do it quickly before the enemy can switch to concentrate on him.

Local numerical advantage in the area around the ball

has always been something that coaches sought, but in recent years the improvement in physical fitness meant that more than ever before, this numerical advantage can only be very temporary.

It can only be obtained by back players pushing forward, and the immediate breakthrough has to be effected quickly (before the enemy can concentrate) and then play should preferably be transferred to another attacking focal point, and numerical advantage gained as quickly as possible in the new zone of operations and before the opponents can reinforce their defence there.

Numerical advantage can be gained by beating an opponent but observation of the best teams of recent years reveals that it is more often gained by defenders and midfield players taking up good support positions, and even sprinting ahead of the strikers.

After the match in Düsseldorf in 1973 when West Germany beat Czechoslovakia 3–0, Helmut Schoen said that we had generally played good football but that our players did not seem to want to score goals. In fact we created only one shooting position, and that was not exploited. Indeed, around that time our national team scored only three goals in seven games.

So we came to reappraise our approach to the game as a whole and resolved to involve not only the full backs but also the two centre backs in attacking situations, even going forward to make goal attempts themselves. To develop this within the team we evolved the system of play in blocks, with the players encouraged and coached, to switch from their own block to another.

Playing to the system: 1–3–3–3, our defensive block consisted of two full backs, a stopper and a *libero*; the midfield block comprised three players, and in the attacking block we had a right winger, a centre forward and a left sided striker who was not a winger.

At the start of a match they would be disposed in three blocks as shown in Diagram 13.

From the outset we laid down several basic principles that were easy to understand, for the two phases of the game:

1. If we were forced to defend, the midfield players would fall back and become part of the defensive block while the attacking players should be ready to drop back, finding space in the midfield block *when we won possession of the ball* in order to make themselves easy to find.

2. If we were able to start an attack, the midfield block moved forward with the attacking block, while the defensive block moved quickly up to the halfway

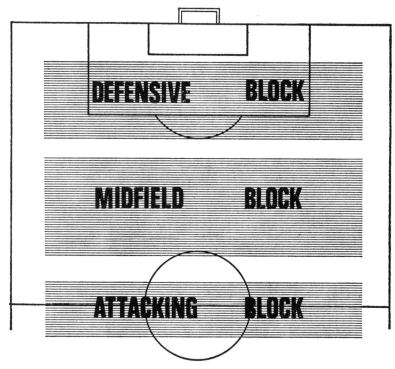

Diagram 13

line, in order to keep the team compact so that back players could quickly go forward to transfer into the midfield and even attacking block, if and when the opportunity arose.

It was also understood that when, after concentrating in defence, we began a counter-attack, the defensive block moved out to the halfway line as fast as possible. This meant that any opponent left behind was offside and out of the game. It also kept the team compact and gave the back players the same attacking opportunities as in 2 above.

Now we had the problem of coaching the players to go forward from one block to another.

Commencing with the defensive phase of the game we had our players disposed according to their positions in Diagram 13, and using other players in the squad we provided opposition using four other players in the defensive block, three opponents in midfield, and three more in attack.

We began by giving the ball to a player in the defensive block and instructing the defensive players only to play keep-ball against their four opponents in the defensive zone which was marked out as in the diagram by traffic cones.

After only a few moments, and judging the time right— just before a defender was about to receive the ball—I blew my whistle.

At this signal, the player receiving the ball had to look up and pass to a player in the midfield block, or the attacking block. Then, having made his pass, he had immediately to sprint out and join the midfield block. Simultaneously, the closest player in the midfield block (to the man in possession now), had to make a run forward into the attacking block angling his run so that he entered the zone of immediate play and made himself available to receive a pass.

From there the attacking players attempted to create a shooting position and score, with myself and my good friend and colleague Dr Jozef Venglos, calling advice to the players re where to run, and where to give the ball. Hopefully, the attack developed to a shooting position, and when the attack was concluded or broke down, I blew my whistle again, and at that signal, each of the players trotted back to re-position in his block, and off we went again, as in Diagram 14.

In this way, each of the defensive players was forced to come out in turn, even the *libero*.

At the next stage, after the back players had become

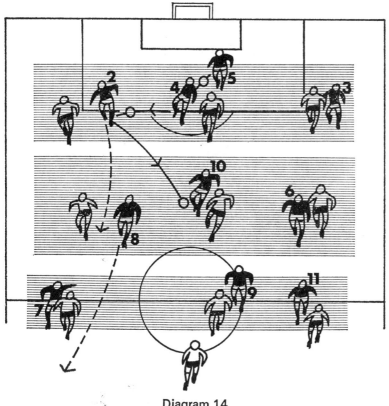

Diagram 14

accustomed to going forward and the midfield block players were making intelligent runs upfield, we changed our basic approach.

We still began by playing keep-ball in our defensive zone, but now the signal was to call the name of a player in the defensive block. Immediately his name was called he had to sprint out into the midfield block, and the player with the ball had to find him with a good pass. From there the ball went forward with the player from the defensive block helping in every way to develop the attack, even going forward, ahead of the attacking block in search of a penetrating pass. This is outlined in Diagram 15.

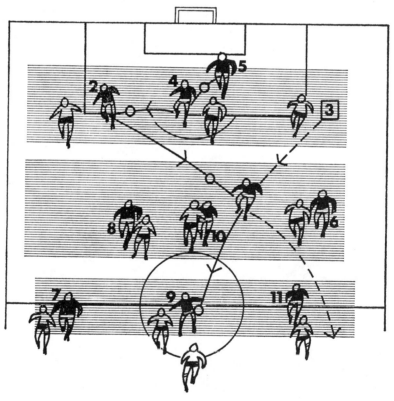

Diagram 15

Right from the start we were quite successful at this aspect of the game for every player would like above all to attack, which is the real enjoyment in the game, with goalscoring the climax that everyone seeks by the nature of the game. Thus the back players needed little encouragement to come out and help in attack.

Our *libero*, Anton Ondrus, had already been doing this successfully in club games. A player with a great deal of skill for a big man, and very good in the air, he became one of our key players in every phase of the game, and was acclaimed by all international critics.

We still continued this practice with defensive players coming out to join the other blocks, but once the players knew what was required from them, we also began to work on the midfield block.

As in Diagram 16, the three midfield players played keep-ball in their block, again marked out by traffic cones. After a few moments of inter passing I again blew my whistle, and the man receiving the ball now had to look up, find an attacking player well positioned on the flanks with a good pass that could be screened from the man marking him—and then sprint forward, moving inside or outside the man he had given the ball to, as shown by the arrows in the Diagram, but taking care not to run offside.

As soon as I had blown my whistle, I then called to one of the players in the defensive block by name, and he had to come out into the midfield block to support the man who now had the ball (the striker), in case he needed to play the ball back. In that case, the defender who had come out should be well placed to find the man running from midfield with an accurate pass and set an attack going in its final phase.

After each midfield player had been coached to go forward in this way two or three times, we again reverted to the system of calling upon a player by name. Thus, as

Diagram 16

one of the midfield players, player 8 in Diagram 17, was about to receive the ball, I called the name of player number 10, and while player 8 had to find one of the players in the attacking block, player 10 from the midfield block had to sprint forward and make a run into a position where he could receive a pass and break through, for example as shown by the arrows in the Diagram.

Now we had players from the defensive block moving forward at two different signals to reinforce the midfield block, and we also had, at the same kind of signals, midfield players sprinting forward to join the attacking block. The final touch was to get players from the defensive

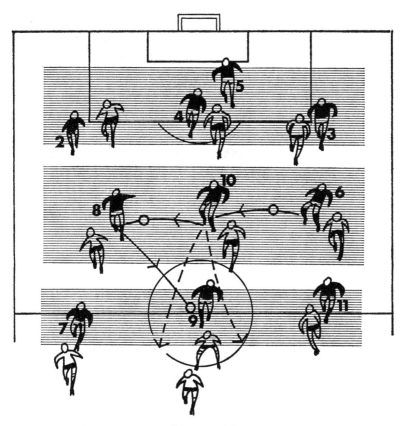

Diagram 17

block to go through the midfield block and on into the attacking block. This we did in two stages.

With four v. four in the defensive block; three v. three in the midfield block and three v. three in the attacking block, we began in defence and midfield playing separate keep-ball games. Then at a signal, whistling or calling a name alternately, one of the defenders came out into the midfield block to make it four against three there.

We let the keep-ball game go on in midfield for a very short period, then made the signals that prompted a midfield player to find an attacking player with a pass, and immediately called the name of the defender. Immediately his name was called, on the right, in the centre or down the left according to his defensive position, and try to receive a pass and help organise a breakthrough . . . as in Diagrams 18 and 19 for the right and left flanks. This was especially important on our left flank for we had no left winger and we relied a great deal on left back Koloman Gogh moving up very often to try and play a leading role in pressing attacks down the left.

Exactly *how* we were to try and effect a breakthrough we learned a lot from observation of the best teams in the 1972 European Championship and the play of

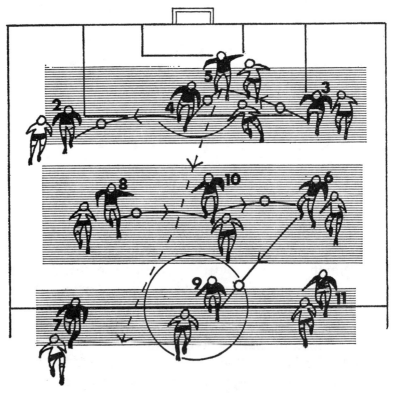

Diagram 18

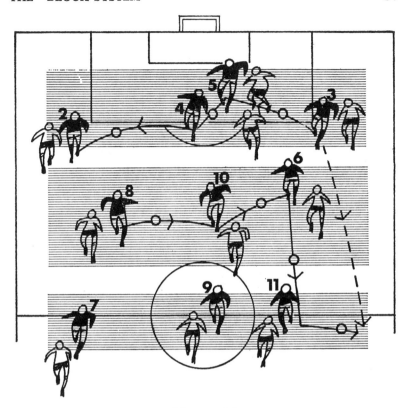

Diagram 19

Holland, West Germany and Poland in the 1974 World Cup.

All these teams frequently used two players on the wing to break through, which we call "doubling" in Czechoslovakia, but is known as overlapping in Britain and by other words elsewhere.

By these methods, assuming we were quick enough in transforming our team from defence into attack, we managed to concentrate two players on the wings against one full back.

We had some problems at first because by their nature, and by tradition, the game in Czechoslovakia has been based on short passing with the emphasis on safety, in the sense that the players were encouraged to play short "safe" passes that would guarantee we did not lose possession of the ball.

This meant inevitably that our attacks built up slowly by comparison with the most prominent teams. We did not have the kind of player who is accustomed to hitting accurate passes over longer distances of up to 40 or 50 yards. But with great efforts by the coaches of our leading clubs, and above all by the players themselves, we managed eventually to develop a team by 1976 that was much more "international" in character.

After a great deal of work, coaching the players in playing to the block system, we were finally able to maintain, most of the time, a defensive block before our own penalty area, when necessary, a block of 7 to 9 players. But when we broke out to attack we were also able to build a midfield block very rapidly of up to 8 players, and in the final attacking phase we often managed to create a block of 6 to 8 players in and around the enemy penalty area.

So we were able to build a team that was quite successful against opponents who played a positive attacking game, by counter-attacking. But against an opponent who played defensively, our attacks had to be more complex. In this case, the duty of the players in the attacking block was to keep on the move, thus taking their markers out of position and creating space for midfield players, one of the full backs and the *libero* to come forward and use that space. In particular this was important when we had reached the enemy penalty area, as well as in the build up to goal, and movement across the field or in diagonal directions were most effective because they stretched the enemy defenders in depth, but most importantly in width.

But in all cases we tried most of all to penetrate the opposing defence by play on the wings where it is comparatively easy to "double" or even if there are two defenders, to gain a local numerical advantage and still break through.

Having gone round the line of defenders by penetrating on the flanks, we stressed the importance in the final phase of attack, on trying to reach the enemy goal line and then with a reverse pass, try to find a colleague who is well positioned to shoot. This player might even be our stopper or *libero*, so that on occasions it may be a full back who penetrates to the goal line, and another defender who receives the reverse pass on or near the edge of the penalty area and shoots.

It was essential that the players in the attacking block drop back to join the midfield block as an attack built up, and for back players to go forward and join the attacking block as we pressed our attacks. All our coaching was concentrated on these two priorities above all.

For this of course we needed players who were able to play well in two or more positions. But we also needed the right balance in the team of players with different qualities, as we have seen from other successful teams.

These types of player can be characterised as follows:
(a) creative players
(b) players with "fighting qualities"
(c) players who were a blend of the two above
(d) outstanding personality players

Our team of 1976 was comprised of the following types of player given in the team formation:

		P in goal		
		C		
O		F		F
	O	F	C	
C		F	O	

In the above team the letters indicate their style of play thus:

P: Personality player

C: Creative player

F: a "fighter" type

O: players with both creative ability and fighting qualities.

It will perhaps be of interest to note some statistical evidence obtained from analysing a film of the 1976 European Championship final against West Germany.

In many ways our play still followed the traditional lines with 78 % of our passes over distances up to 20 yards. But the remaining 22 % of our passes were over middle to long distances which was a great improvement, and overall 86 % of our passes reached the player aimed for and thus allowed our attack to continue.

But the biggest improvement in our overall performance was in our attacking play with no less than 41 passes aimed at colleagues in and around the penalty area that put a player in a shooting or heading position from which he might have scored. These passes were given by Masny, our right winger (9 such passes); Panenka (midfield) with 5 final passes, and even the *libero* Ondrus made 4 such passes.

Most significantly, every outfield player figured in this total, even left back Gogh with 2 final passes, proving that we had successfully involved the entire team in our attacking play.

Other statistics prove that we also increased our players' finishing abilities by a considerable degree. In the final against West Germany our players made 28 goal attempts of which 19 were the result of quick counter-attacks of the type we had worked on.

In the semi-final against Holland our players made 18 goal attempts of which 12 came after the type of attacking moves we had worked on.

It should not be thought that we employed our defenders in attack without ensuring the defence against a quick counter-attack by the opponent. In all cases where for example, our *libero* or stopper moved upfield, one of the midfield players had to drop back and fulfil his role temporarily. Similarly, if our opponents employed two wingers, then whenever a full back moved upfield, a midfield player dropped back to mark his winger temporarily. From the 1973–74 season until 1976 we had a settled team, and before the most important games we had up to fourteen days in which to work together and prepare the players.

The work rate of the players improved to a considerable degree above the general level in Czech football, and by concentrating our coaching and playing in blocks, our basic 1–3–3–3 team plan became very flexible.

In the attacking phase we often had a formation of 1–2–3–4 or 1–2–2–5 and sometimes 2–4–4 giving us an attacking block of seven or eight players. On the other hand, when forced to defend we frequently had our players disposed to a 1–5–3–1 formation or even 1–5–4–0 giving eight or nine players in defence.

The tactical formations above are reinforced by statistical evidence from our final against West Germany in 1976.

For example, right winger Masny made 20 defensive interventions when our attacks broke down. Even more successful was our attacking midfield player Moder who made 33 defensive interventions.

According to my experience, coaching the players to play in blocks helps to develop multi-purpose players.

If we consider first the attacking block, the three players concerned were responsible for 28% of the challenges offered to opponents who had the ball in the semi-final against Holland and final against West Germany. This was a big improvement, reflecting the fact that when our attacks broke down, the players in the attacking block fell back to reinforce the midfield block. There was also a marked improvement by players from the midfield block who consciously made every effort to join the attacking block when we had possession. They were so successful that Moder from the midfield block scored three of our four goals against the Soviet Union in the quarter-finals, with another midfield player Panenka getting the other goal in an aggregate 4–2 success (2–0 and 2–2).

The other midfield player Dobias was also very successful in the last two games in Yugoslavia. Against Holland in the semi-final he laid on the final passes from which we scored two goals, and against West Germany he scored the second goal himself.

Overall, the coaching of players in blocks did not restrict their individual initiative but did enlarge the radius of activity of each player and enormously improved their positional play "off the ball".

By coaching and playing in blocks we improved the effectiveness of our team for the eleven individuals brought their own qualities and skills, their morale and will-to-win, and by playing in more than one block they improved the level of the team performance.

This was proved by the number of times that enemy attacks broke down because of intervention by players from our attacking block and midfield block and was in direct contrast to the way in which the team played in the period 1972–73—before the decision to work and play in blocks was taken.

In practice however, the success of our team still hinged on the ability of the players to adapt their play, their willingness to master the techniques of playing in a block other than their own, and on their achieving the optimum physical fitness and will-to-win.

Finally, I would like everyone to recall that none of the four teams in the 1976 European Championship semi-finals played with blatantly defensive tactics and there was no case of serious foul play. Although it may in time be forgotten, if Czechoslovakia were the winners of the trophy, everyone in Yugoslavia, and indeed a television audience of hundreds of millions, were agreed at the time that the real winner was the game of football.

5/ The Development of Hungarian Football Since 1953-54

by **Lajos Baroti**

Lajos Baroti was born at Szeged on 19th August 1914. As a player he spent his entire career with his first club, the local First Division team Szeged. Baroti was always a right half, playing first class football for 16 years and gained two full caps for Hungary.

As a coach he worked with several junior teams before having a spell in charge of his old club, but really made a name for himself in Budapest with Ujpest Dozsa. He took over there in 1968, leading the club to the championship in 1969–70, and with the Hungarians changing their season, they then took Cup and League doubles in three consecutive seasons from 1969 to 1971.

In the championship, Baroti stayed on to guide the club to three more successes, making it six championships in a row. He then left to take over Peru's national team for a spell while the team he had built brought even more successes in the Hungarian League for Ujpest Dozsa.

At international level, Hungary never failed to qualify in a World Cup competition with Baroti in charge. In 1958 he took Hungary to the World Cup final rounds and in 1962 he led Hungary to Chile. He was still in charge when they reached the last 16 in 1966, but was with Ujpest Dozsa for the next two series.

By 1975, The Hungarian FA had realised that their game had fallen behind and they appointed Lajos Baroti to rebuild their national team in a modern style. He did just that, and steered them once more to the World Cup finals in Argentina.

The traditional Hungarian game was established firmly on superb technique, and total mastery of the ball. Their play reached a superlative peak when Hungary beat England 6–3 at Wembley in 1953, the first foreign team to beat England at home, and they underlined their supremacy by again beating England, this time by seven goals to one, in Budapest a few months later.

Since then, however, the face of the modern game has been changed and neglecting physical qualities, with their fans and coaches convinced that ball control was everything, the Hungarian game suffered and their national team began to flounder against the world's best.

Lajos Baroti looks back over the years of change and explains how the Hungarians at last began to bring their style of play up to date. Under his guidance the Hungarian game regained some of its past lustre and here Mr Baroti explains in detail how the revolution in Hungarian football was achieved.

The whole conception of the Hungarian game has had to be changed since the 1950's because the opposition today would simply not allow anyone to play as Ferenc Puskas and his colleagues played twenty-five years ago. Football today is a very different game.

Around the period of Hungary's golden era, say 1952 to 1955, the game was based on the maxims: control, look, pass. Players with good skills were allowed to pull the ball down, look around for a colleague to pass to and meanwhile they showed off their tricks with the ball.

In the changing game we have seen over the last fifteen years a new kind of skill has been developed, for opponents do not give you time or space in which to play the old way. Today the opposition is putting pressure on you all the time.

Making the change was difficult for Hungarians to accept, for the Central European School of football has always been based on ball skills, improvisation and clever solutions to problems posed by opponents.

At the other extreme today we have the Western European style, particularly the game played in Britain where football is like a fight, a battle all the time. The Hungarian football public would never accept the British style of play even now.

So we have had to compromise in modernising the Hungarian game.

For years, fans and coaches in Hungary talked about the "wunderteam" or Golden Team as the 1953–54 side are known in Hungary. But that has tied everyone down more than a little because everyone felt that they must follow in the footsteps of Puskas & Co., and continue to play the same type of game.

However, this style of play really had become outdated for in those days an average player would run about 2,000 yards in a ninety minute game while today the modern player is required to run more like 6,000 yards in each game.

Not only running for 6,000 yards now, but sprinting flat out for a great part of the time.

While other countries were adapting their training methods to enable their players to play in this new style, in Hungary we were still coaching in the old-fashioned way, and that was very largely why we failed to qualify for the World Cup in 1970 and again in 1974.

Even in 1966 when we qualified for the World Cup staged in England we were still trying to play to the old Puskas style, though at a faster pace. Other coaches took over the national team after that but they all failed because they were still working more or less in the same old way.

Certainly it would be wrong to blame the players for Hungary's failures around that time. It was the coaches who were to blame, but even there it is hard to criticise them because they were under really severe pressure to retain the old standards, by both the press and the public.

I would say that in Hungary now we have a dual approach as far as coaching is concerned.

At club level, with a squad of only 16 or 18 players at his disposal, the tactical thinking of the coach and his way of preparing the players in training must be determined by the various talents and abilities available to him.

The coach of the national team however has the opportunity to develop his own ideas and with the entire country to choose from, he can restrict himself to picking only players who can fit in with his plans.

There has also been a big change in our physical preparations since 1970, for after our failure to qualify for the World Cup in that year, the top coaches were called together by the Hungarian Football Association for a special conference. The whole approach of the Hungarian game to the World Cup was re-examined and we realised that our players fell very far behind the leading countries in terms of physical preparation.

In this field it is now very much easier for the Hungarian national team coach than in many other countries. After that conference, the Football Association worked out physical training schedules and distributed them to all the leading clubs.

These training schedules made it compulsory for all the coaches to work according to the programme. It was acceptable because it didn't interfere with tactical plans or coaching in other fields like technique, but simply laid down a basic minimum physical training programme that every player had to complete every week.

This directive was designed to improve the speed and stamina of the Hungarian players, bringing them up to the level attained elsewhere. The programme included work with weights and also physical exercises specially designed to improve the dynamic strength of the players' leg muscles. Thus the physical condition of the top Hungarian players was brought up to the point where it compared favourably with that of any opposition—even including England for example.

Before this directive went out to the clubs it was quite usual for the Hungarian national team to play very well in the first half or at least the opening 35 minutes. But too many games were lost in the second half when the players "blew out" with physical exhaustion. The players were able to raise the pace of their game to match their opponents but only for a limited period. But this extra physical effort took its toll later in the game.

We have changed our basic approach in other ways too. In the old days the players stood still during ball practice— waiting for the ball to arrive. Now for example, everything is done at a much faster pace and all skills are practised with the players receiving the ball whilst on the move.

Naturally I also had new ideas about the kind of team I wanted to develop. I wanted to create a squad of 15 or 16 players and keep them together. I told them at regular intervals, that the national team would be chosen exclusively from them, in order to encourage them.

I also had a new conception of how I wanted them to play and to this end I worked out eight basic practices with the ball that every player must become familiar with.

I got my players to practise them, repeating them over and over again. The most important objective here was to get them to make creative runs *off the ball* in a variety of given situations.

But these basic practices only gave the players the outline of how I wanted them to play—the individual was left free to use his initiative and introduce variations in match play. But in training I wanted the basic moves carried out exactly.

All these basic moves were carried out repeatedly, but once the players understood what was required of them, every practice was carried out under match-like conditions —at top speed and with live opposition. In this way the practices were made realistic and the players were always under pressure.

In the past, Hungarian players would go through a programme of 25 or 30 skill practices without opposition. The players perfected their technique and in training were able to perform as if giving an exhibition of skill. But in match play the coaches were surprised to find that all too often the players' skill broke down under pressure from opponents.

With the eight basic practices the players go through each one perhaps 25 or 30 times in each training session, so that the way I want them to play, as seen in these combined skill practices with the ball, eventually become habit.

Although I am opposed to the ideas of some Hungarian coaches I still believe in the practice of technique in the right conditions: skills carried out quickly, on the move and with opposition. Skills like heading, passing and overall control.

I also do a lot of work at the skills I believe each individual player should be especially good at, according to his usual playing position and what I require him to do in matches.

In terms of team selection I have confined myself to a

squad of 16 players (maximum) at any given time for I believe that it takes a period of about three or four years to develop a really good international team, as distinct from a club side.

The Hungarians in 1953 and West Germans in 1974 were I believe, successful, at least to some degree because they had kept a more or less settled side for three or four years. In that time all the players got to know each other, and how they will play, really well.

If you can keep a settled side for three or four years or more then it invariably means that you have a good team.

If the coach or manager keeps making changes it is clear that the team are not playing well. In some teams, at certain periods, it may be that no one knows who will play in the next international, and clearly this is a sign of weakness.

To my way of thinking and working, if you have a player who is perhaps less good a player, less skilled than some others, the fact that he is accustomed to playing with those around him—and the others with him—makes him more valuable than a new player.

This applies particularly with a national team and the way that I have worked, for no matter how good a player may be, a new man will not be familiar with my basic practices, and his part in each of them. Neither will he be aware of our varying approaches to set-piece situations both in attack and defence.

So even though a new player may be much better as an individual, the coach cannot keep going back to the ABC for the benefit of new players so it is just not practical to bring in new players all the time.

Because the framework of the team revolved around my basic practices our play had to be stereotyped to some degree. In the national team I try to get my players to play the same way all the time. If at any particular period we did become stereotyped we invariably found that opponents who might anticipate what we were going to do next were overtaken by events, because we did everything too fast, or because one particular player introduced a variation.

The only adjustments we made came because for example, our opponents had some outstanding star. Then we would put one of our players on that star to mark him tight.

But in my philosophy you have to play *your game* and impose it on the opposition. If you fail to do this, it means that they have imposed their game on you and you will find that you are under pressure and defending too much.

With the Hungarian team I played with two wingers and a centre forward, for I believe there cannot be truly attacking football without two wingers. I also want my right back and right midfield to utilise space that crops up on the right flank, and the left midfield and left back to take advantage of space that appears in front of them—utilising this space to attack.

With regard to my eight basic practices it took my first squad about one year for all the players to become familiar with them. We never trained together without practising these exercises. But that squad included two players, Tibor Nyilasi and Laszlo Pusztai, who were real stars and were able to vary the game at will if they saw something good.

The reason why I attach so much importance to the basic practices is that they give the players ideas about running *off the ball* in support of the man in possession. After a long period of practice in this way, the man on the ball often had as many as four or five team-mates to whom he could pass.

Before that, thinking in the old Puskas terms, football

was a game for individuals, whereas now, it has become a team game in the fullest sense.

A coach can only work on a general scheme of things to prepare his players. Once his men are out on the pitch it is up to the players, and the coach can only provide a general framework within which eleven individuals can play as a team. It is up to each player to read situations for himself and make decisions.

Overall the aim now must be to have a numerical advantage over your opponents wherever the ball goes, whether you are attacking or forced to defend.

This advantage can only be achieved if defenders move up to support the attack, and if, in their turn, the forwards drop back to help when the opposition applies pressure on our goal.

That is why stamina is so important today, for the players must be able to run at varying speeds for the whole ninety minutes if necessary. If I have to put a finger on just one point of modern football it is the ability to outnumber the opposition in the area around the ball at at all times. That determines the difference between success and failure.

After I had been in charge of the Hungarian national team for about a year and a half we met Greece and the Soviet Union in the 1978 World Cup qualifying competition.

Bearing in mind the opposition I selected 16 players and told them they would stay together for all four games.

We had regular training sessions together before these games, working at my basic practices and generally conveying my ideas about the game to the players. The players knew that competition for places was limited to just those 16 and that made them more relaxed and confident which also helped a lot.

But our regular training sessions and the 16 man limit

also enabled me to develop the vitally important mutual trust between the coach and his players.

Limited to 16 players it was quite easy to give the players ideas for free kicks—passes and shots from free kick situations. To bring in new players would have meant starting again, and old members of the group would have got bored going over old ground for the benefit of newcomers.

In general terms some players who were both very skilful and very popular had to be omitted from the squad because they could not adapt their play to the needs of modern football.

Every good player must be able to beat an opponent, but it is only effective and necessary at the right time and if it is in the interests of the team as a whole.

For example, how can you continually achieve numerical advantage if someone keeps losing the ball through trying unsuccessfully to beat a man? That only leads to a lot of hard and unnecessary running for the entire team.

Today we must have team players with talent. There is only one place for those players who play for themselves or to please the crowd: amongst the spectators.

Ten years ago there was no conception of a luxury player. Someone who could do clever tricks with the ball and beat men to no particular advantage to their team were regarded as stars. Now, those who dribble unnecessarily are widely accepted in Hungary as luxury players.

We want good team players now, gifted team players, for I repeat, all good players should be able to beat a man when the need arises.

In a four v. four situation when our team is attacking, sometimes the only way to achieve a numerical advantage is to eliminate one of the four defenders to make it four versus three. In such situations the man on the ball must be able to beat a man, but then give a quick pass to the extra man who has just been set free.

Mental attitude is also important today. I like to pick players who hate to lose a game; who feel they must win the match, players that feel they MUST score a goal when we are losing. Such players are vital, and successful teams must have players with this mental streak in them.

The public always likes to see a team that has the will to win and when they feel it, the fans get behind the players and encourage them and urge them on. That happened when we played against the Soviet Union in Budapest in the 1978 World Cup. The whole team had belief in themselves and confidence that they would win, and this enthusiasm and confidence spread to the crowd and the fans urged the players on—so it works both ways.

This was especially important for a Hungarian crowd with memories of Puskas & Co. for when international players fail to match up to the old heroes, they are showered with sarcastic remarks from the spectators.

Another thing about Hungarian spectators, though perhaps this is not limited to Hungary, the crowd expects certain standards from the players. The public know that the top players are better paid than the average fan and they expect clever tricks and above all a winning team. If they are not satisfied in one respect or the other the fans become jealous of the higher standard of living the players have and again start to be sarcastic and shout insults.

But in my philosophy, winning alone is not everything. Winning by hook or by crook brings me no joy. I want my team to win with style. To achieve that, all the players from goalkeeper to outside left must share my feelings and beliefs—they have to have the will to win and win well— with style.

In Hungary particularly, the fans want it too, and if they get anything less the crowd loses patience with the players. So for us the first essential is to play attractive, attacking football and to try and be constructive for the whole ninety minutes—with every player working.

Some journalists who have seen the national team training are critical of my eight basic passing and combined practices, arguing that it will lead to stereotyped and predictable play.

But the fans do not "see" the basic moves, and neither do the journalists who have not watched us train. All they see are good passing moves resulting in a shot at goal, or even a goal. Even if we reproduce one straight from our training ground four or five times in one game the fans do not remember that they have seen the same move before, they simply fail to recognise what we are doing.

In any case what are we doing? These basic schemes are strictly applied only in training and are used to teach the players where to position, where they ought to sprint to when we have the ball, and also where they should try to get back to when we lose the ball.

The new Hungarian style is based on much faster football with players who have the will to win and are very combative. The change was made around 1975-76 and now, even those fans who wanted to see a new 1954-style team are satisfied with good football at a faster speed, allied to success.

But for me the biggest single change that has been effected is that the best of the new Hungarian players do not fear physical contact—as they once did.

In training it makes sense to practice the type of football you want your players to play in matches. We have two wingers and we want them to hit the goal line as often as possible. From there they can cross the ball or pull it back depending on the situation.

If the defending side has a big strong goalkeeper who is good in the air plus three big defenders all highly skilled at heading and all well positioned, then it is a gift to the defence if you put a high ball in there. So in that situation you must pull the ball back for someone to shoot at goal.

It is not easy to get your wingers to the goal line repeatedly but that is what we try to do. But once there, the winger has created an ideal situation because the defenders are facing their own goal and are "blind" to attacking players taking up good positions in and around the penalty area.

In training I like to see many one v. one situations on the wings—much better than two v. three defenders in the middle.

Football is generally a passing game today but you cannot take away individuality. The player must know when to pass and when to dribble.

If a player receives the ball when he has an opponent tight on his back then he must pass first time or get kicked. You have to accept that as fact nowadays.

But if the player has space to turn with the ball or receives the ball at his feet when facing the enemy goal, these are situations when you can dribble (if there is not a good pass open to you) because to eliminate the defender on the player with the ball, helps to get numerical superiority around the ball.

In that situation, having beaten your immediate opponent, another defender must leave his man to come across and cover your direct path to goal.

Overall, perhaps the best team players today are those who make good passes in midfield but who, given the ball at their feet in the enemy penalty area, have the skill and courage to dribble.

That is a formula that brings 80% of the goals scored all over the world.

And in tactical terms there is only one over-riding factor. The ideal team will drop back to defend as one unified unit and then, on regaining possession of the ball, will go forward and attack—again as one unit—irrespective of the numbers on the backs of the players.

The basic practices to which I introduced my players were designed to give them an idea of the kind of way I wanted them to play. One of these practices is described in Diagram 20.

All I did was think about the game and sketch out on paper what I consider to be typical modern attacks. The move in Diagram 20 can be carried out starting with the goalkeeper passing to both the right back and the left back and after the early passes, the break can be made down the right flank. Of course they should all be practised many times if this is the way that you want your team to play.

Generally I want my players to make their passes on the ground and this is always relatively easy, building up an attack in your own half of the field. But if an opponent happens to be standing in the way and could cut out the pass that the player wants to make, then of course the ball has to be chipped over the head of the enemy so that he has no chance to intercept and start a counter-attack.

With longer type passes up the middle for a striker to run on to, or for a ball crossed into the goalmouth for headers it is different. In both these situations there will be opponents in the way and to eliminate them and make sure the pass will not be intercepted, the ball has to be lifted well over their heads.

Thus in Diagram 20, the goakeeper throws the ball out —along the ground—to the centre back 5 who controls the ball and turns. The centre back passes to the inside left, withdrawn into midfield, and as he looks up I want my left winger to make a speedy break down the left touchline, trying to take his opponent by surprise. Now player 10 must place a good through pass inside the enemy

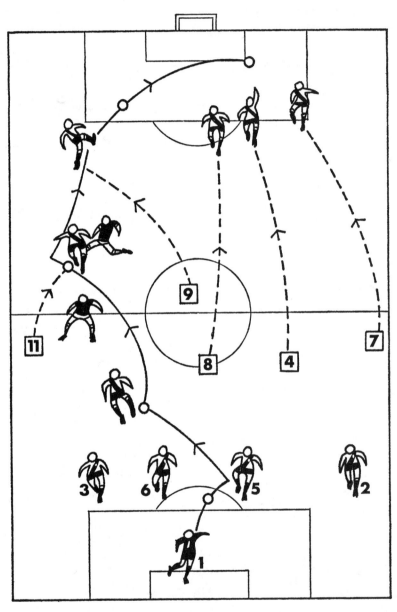

Diagram 20

full back, or hit it over the defender's head. At all events it has to be there for the left winger to run on to and pick up in his stride.

As the left winger runs with the ball, one of the opposing defenders must come across to challenge him, covering for the right back who has been beaten. As this defender moves out to cover, I want my centre forward, player 9, to make a blind side run, moving behind the back of the covering defender and timing his run so that he is not offside. At just the right time, long before the covering player can challenge or player 9 can run offside, I want the left winger to release a good pass for his colleague 9.

Player 9 now looks up with the ball at his feet, while right winger 7, at least two midfield players (4 and 8) and maybe even the right back 2 and centre back 5 or 6, have sprinted hard to take up positions inside the penalty area. There, according to the situation they can try to score with a header at goal; try to head the ball down for a colleague to shoot, or take the ball on their chest and try to volley the ball into goal.

I made my players rehearse this basic practice very many times, and in fact we scored a goal precisely in that way during our World Cup qualifying win against the Soviet Union in Budapest.

But if I made the players practise this move repeatedly, it was not only the movement of the ball that I wanted. While each practice was going on, I was out on the ground with them, talking to the players in turn, telling them where they ought to be at every stage as the movement develops. Of course it was nice to get a goal that way, but the real purpose of the practice was to give me the chance to coach the players *off the ball* at every stage.

Thus when the goalkeeper had the ball I shouted to all the back four players to get themselves into space so that they could receive a ball thrown to them. Then, after the ball was thrown to player 5 (as I had previously ordered), I was shouting at players 4, 8 and 10, as well as right winger 7, to drop back looking for a pass, each one getting himself unmarked.

Working in this way, I hoped that in matches the players would offer themselves for a pass when the centre backs had the ball.

Then when the pass was made from 5 to 10, I called to midfield players 8 and 4 to show themselves to 10, looking for a pass. I also insisted that players 3 (the left back) and 6 (the centre back) come upfield to offer themselves in support.

If that happened in match conditions then player 10 had the choice of four men to pass to, as well as the centre forward (who was involved in other practices in which he received a pass from midfield), and the left winger. But here I wanted the ball played for the left winger 11 to make a break. As player 11 raced away after the pass, I wanted the centre forward to move out left, but he knew that already. So I could concentrate on talking to the other players.

With 11 away on the left I wanted player 10 to seek space inside him, and players 8 and 4 to advance too. I also wanted the right back 2 to go forward, and the left back 3 to follow up in a supporting position in case the winger ran into trouble and wanted an easy ball to play.

So while the players knew in advance exactly what passing movement I wanted from them, I was very busy working with the other players at every stage of the attack.

Of course I could not talk to five players at once, so at first I concentrated on just one or two, as we repeated the practice. Later as these two got to know what I wanted from them, I switched to working with other players, talking to them and telling them where they ought to be and what they should be looking for.

If you do not have very much coaching experience and want some ideas for basic practices, watch very closely one of the professional teams whose play you admire and note down on paper, exactly how they build up their attacks from start to finish.

Note down at least six different ways that your favourite team attacks, and then draw a diagram of the first one for your players before going out onto the training ground to practise it.

Insist that they work at the same attack without opposition, until everyone knows exactly what he must do. At this stage, the coach should tell each player what to do in advance, until everyone directly involved is completely familiar with his role.

Then the coach can switch his efforts to coaching the players not involved as I have described, talking to the players off the ball and telling them where you want them to be.

Once you have reached the point where all the players directly involved know exactly what is required from them, you can now pass on to the second basic practice, and start all over again. Everything will be different now, so each player has to react differently, but if you want them to play the game according to the way you see it and want it played, then you must practise it, and coach *all* the players to help them to do it.

In matches, you might well find that your team carries out the moves you have practised exactly, but that does not matter for the attack will develop too fast for your opponents to realise what is happening. And if you have good intelligent players with good skills, they will vary the basic moves anyway by introducing variations to the play.

Finally, there is one thing that I should stress. Although I have said that all good players should be able to beat a man, if a particular player finds that he is being marked by an opponent who stops him every time he gets the ball, then that player must first of all try to get away from his opponent into a new zone of the pitch, perhaps switching with a colleague, but whatever happens he must stop trying to dribble past a man who can stop him and dispossess him. This must be accepted because every time we get the ball, seven or eight of our players are running hard, expending valuable energy to take up good attacking positions. When the ball is lost in a dribble, all these players now have to run hard to take up defensive positions and quite apart from it being basically stupid to go on trying to beat an opponent who is too good for you or too quick for you, the fact is that by trying to dribble and losing the ball you are making your colleagues run needlessly.

The rule is that if you find you cannot beat a particular opponent then make a simple pass quickly, then sprint away to take up another good position and be content to play a much more limited part in the game than would be the case if you were marked by a man whom you could beat nine times out of ten.

6/ "Pressing Football"

by **Rinus Michels**

Rinus Michels was born in Amsterdam on 9th February 1928. As a player he began with Ajax in 1946, playing first as a centre forward and switching later to inside forward.

He retired in 1958 to earn his living as a teacher of physical education, working at different schools each day. Later he worked as a specialist with deaf children, applying his knowledge to provide physical therapy.

At the same time Michels was working as a coach with an Amsterdam amateur team for six years and in 1965 was offered, and accepted, the post of coach to Ajax. In 1971 he joined CF Barcelona, winning the Spanish championship once but failing to reproduce the magic qualities of the football played by Ajax.

In 1974, Michels perhaps achieved his ultimate in terms of quality football with Holland when, just a few weeks before the 1974 World Cup, he took over the team at short notice to lead them to the final, producing a brand of football that is still talked about even now.

Pressing football is the name by which Rinus Michels describes the game he developed while coach of Ajax Amsterdam, steering them into a position where they were acknowledged as the masters of Europe, and admired by everyone. Journalists tagged the Ajax style TOTAL FOOTBALL, but Michels throws this back in their faces. That is

journalese for what is simply, *real football*, but carried to
its ultimate because they were forever attacking.

Like coaches everywhere, Michels acknowledges that
his conception of *pressing football* was limited on the field
by a shortage of really top class players, even in the Ajax
super-team. For this reason, Michels believes that it was
with the Dutch national team in the 1974 World Cup that
he came closest to achieving the ultimate, because he had
more top quality players at his disposal. Rinus Michels
describes in this chapter how his conception of pressing
football developed gradually until he sat back and thought
it all out to its logical conclusion. He also describes how
he set about creating his ideal style of play though
coaches everywhere would be wise to be cautious.

The conception of pressing football is fabulous, opening up a picture of the game even more attractive and
entertaining than the super-Ajax at their best. But to play
pressing football demands above all, a squad of at least
fifteen players who have a wide range of top quality
skills and in addition are highly intelligent in football
terms. On top of that they must be super fit.

No one, not even Ajax, or Holland in 1974 were even
able to field the eleven super players that Michels needed
to see the fulfilment of his ideas. Coaches of lesser teams
can therefore learn from this chapter, picking out aspects
of the game that they can coach, and perhaps use one or
two of Michels' coaching ideas, but they should not try
to play pressing football unless they really have enough
super-stars, with at least three and preferably four of the
players, all-time greats.

To try and play pressing football with lesser players will
lead to disaster for it is an attacking conception that even
Michels, using top grade professional players confesses
can be dangerous, even begging for defeat against counter-
attacking teams.

In modern football we try in training to practise and develop those qualities that the players need to play the game today. But throughout Europe at least, we are hampered by a lack of natural football skills that all good players had in earlier years.

Because the game is changing from moment to moment, the coach must prepare the players for that. But the most difficult problem for modern coaches is the lack of individual skills that earlier generations had, and there is no time to develop individual techniques today when so much emphasis is on team play. This lack of individual ability is clearly demonstrated by the dearth of truly great players.

It is most difficult to create really great football because when the players have won the ball and started a promising move, the opponents are so well prepared physically that they can run and run all day. So they can stay close to players running with the ball, while others tight-mark his colleagues and run all over the place to fill in spaces within their defensive area.

Modern football is epitomised by tight-marking and this makes it very difficult for anyone to play. Allied to tight-marking, better physical preparation presents a dual problem: on the one hand it is becoming every year more difficult for players to develop naturally to the level of skill they had before, and on the other hand, the improved physical condition of players generally makes it impossible for players with a high degree of skill alone, to play their natural game.

So there is a kind of balance. We cannot develop the extremely skilful players we once had—and we couldn't use them even if we had them. Thus we can say that despite all our efforts, football is not improving. Changing, yes, but improving, no.

In the minds of many people, what has been described

as "total football" seems to sum up an idea of the best in football in recent years. But although I was the coach of the team that first presented *total football*, these are not my words; it is not my expression.

The expression "total football" is a product of the press, coined by a journalist. And if I use the expression it is only because I know that the average person will understand what I mean by these words.

But given a choice, I would describe what the journalists call *total football*, as "pressing football". To me, this expression seems to put the emphasis on the type of football I was trying to create with Ajax and with the Dutch national team in the 1974 World Cup.

What I wanted to create was a game in which all ten outfield players pressed forward all the time—even when we didn't have the ball!

When our opponents had the ball we could not press and attack, but the emphasis in the type of football that I envisaged was that even then, all ten outfield players *pressed forward in an attempt to get the ball back*. Now it will be obvious why I prefer the expression "pressing football" because one way or the other we were pressing forward all the time.

If, as I have already said, football is not getting any better, it is nevertheless developing, just as it has always been. Nothing in nature stands still; everything is constantly changing, even though the rate of change may be very slow. In every field of human endeavour, everything is developing, and football cannot be excluded.

You cannot stop the development of football, though according to the ideas of different coaches, it can develop in different ways. But it is always changing, even though the process is very slow and may not be apparent at any given time.

I say the game is changing, but by that I mean on a

world scale. Somewhere, every minute, coaches are getting new ideas, or giving old ideas a new twist. But I must admit that at any given moment in time it is very difficult to see this change clearly. But if you look back over say, ten years, you can see that there has been a big change.

Perhaps the biggest change of recent years has been the new approach to physical preparation.

Physically the best teams are now very well prepared but they are also better prepared tactically and able to mark their opponents more strictly than ever before.

In the middle sixties, there was still plenty of space in which to play football of an attacking, attractive style. But by the middle seventies this space had disappeared.

Because everyone is now so strong they do not let you play today. Each individual player has such a lot of energy that he can run about for the entire ninety minutes and destroy everything an attacking team attempts to do. Today the opposition does not let you play.

This process developed over several years but it can now be seen clearly.

In Europe particularly, each team is now at the peak of its physical preparation, at peak physical form *at the start of the league programme*. But a decade ago, the aim of every coach was to have all his players develop their skills to the highest possible degree of efficiency, while in terms of physical condition the players did not reach their peak until perhaps six weeks to two months into the league programme.

Technical skills are still very important but it is much more difficult to use your skills now. In the middle sixties, a very good technical player was always able to show his talent in a team of good quality. But now, dating approximately from the early seventies in most countries, it was possible that this same player could not play in a First

Division team. Today you need skill and the ability to do everything with the ball very quickly.

A decade ago if you were a skilful player you had space (and therefore time), to give a pass, to make a feint, to beat a man. To show off everything you could do with the ball. But now you have to do even the most simple things very quickly, very often even being forced by tight-marking and quick tackling to make a pass first time.

Many very skilful players who were once able to collect the ball and beat an opponent with a wide variety of tricks are no longer allowed to play. They are eliminated from the game by tight-marking and quick tackling.

What we can call the moment of action with the ball is now very much shorter. So players must be able to carry out their skills very quickly, and this makes it more difficult to play.

So nowadays, even the most brilliant technical players have problems. I know this to be true because I had in the Barcelona team in 1977, players who were so skilful that five years before were amongst the best players in the world. So they had to adapt their play, and those who could not change had to be dropped from the first team.

The most skilful players not only had to adapt their style of play, their manner of expressing their ability with the ball, but they also had to develop the courage to tolerate tight-marking for the entire ninety minutes and to play in spite of quick tackling and a strong physical challenge.

If they did not have the courage for the battle with their tight-marking opponent and the heart to play the game the modern way, then they had to go and make room for someone who could.

The first requirement of the modern game is that when you are tightly marked you must move around off the ball in order to get free from your opponent. When you move you are leaving your opponent behind, but because he is chasing you, the amount of space and time thus gained is very slight indeed. It is in this brief moment, often limited to a fraction of a second, that the modern player has to use his skill either to beat his opponent or to make a pass.

This tight-marking game, with even the strikers charged with tight-marking the defenders marking them (if they try to move up and attack) is quite widespread. West Germany are perhaps the best at it, and in their club teams the system is very clear to see.

So in the moment that my team gains possession of the ball I want all my players to move away from the men marking them, trying to find space to receive the ball. This individual searching for space is very important and is an individual technical quality we must have today. But this has led directly to another change in the collective technique of the team, because overall there is now much more mobility within the team than there ever was before, with all ten outfield players trying to find space and make themselves available to receive a pass.

I have no doubt that players are moving much more during ninety minutes play than they did ten years ago. To watch films of the top teams of ten years ago confirms this theory—that overall mobility within the team is much greater.

This leads directly to the biggest single problem facing the game today. The players are better prepared physically than ever before, and the tactical awareness of the players is much improved and indicated by the greater movement off the ball. So these two factors have combined to make it much more difficult to play football and on top of this, instead of improving in terms of individual technique, which is necessary to play in modern conditions, the modern player is less skilled than his predecessors were.

The game generally is suffering because the players do not have the highly developed skills to match the improved physical preparation and greater tactical understanding. This stems from the fact that young boys between the ages of five and ten years, these very vital years, are not spending as much time playing football as they used to do.

There is no way that players can make up later for these lost five years at the most critical age in their technical development. So although the game has improved in other respects, the level of skill we require today is missing.

With regard to the mobility of the individuals and the team as a whole I began to work on this when I was with Ajax. In my last four years in Amsterdam we began to get very positive results from this work.

When attacking players were tightly marked, they were all attempting to get free by moving into space. In addition, we began to involve defensive players in attacking football, but this was not achieved in one year.

In my last two years with Ajax we had all four back players attacking at different moments. By taking up attacking positions, the back four players helped the attacking players to get free from their opponents; and in addition, with good passes, and at times, shots and headers at goal, the individual defenders often became as dangerous as centre forwards and wingers.

This leads directly to my new conception of the game, developed in the last few years, which I refer to as pressing football, and is revolutionary.

If we look back over recent years in the development of the game we can see some teams that clearly played with a revolutionary conception.

The style of Brazil in the 1958 World Cup was based on the 4–2–4 system. It quickly became popular throughout the world, but at the time, in 1958, it was revolutionary. It was new because it was conceived by the coach.

Another, earlier example of a new conception was provided by the Hungarians who developed their ideas between 1952 and 1954. Their style was based on greater mobility between the attacking players and the midfield players, who moved around with far greater mobility then we had ever seen before. This Hungarian team developed from the ideas of their coach, and again it was based on a new conception of the game.

The system of FC Internazionale (Milan) under Helenio Hererra was a revolutionary way of playing too. Like the Brazilian's 4–2–4 before it, the Inter system was widely copied.

Each of the teams I have mentioned brought a new conception to the game based on the ideas of their coach. They had very clear ideas about how they wanted their teams to play, and they coached their players to reproduce the style of play they wanted.

"Pressing football" is based on a conception of the game that is entirely new, very different from anything we had seen in the game before 1974.

As with all revolutionary conceptions of the game, it did not develop overnight. It began with the attacking ideas I coached with Ajax, but pressing football really started with the 1974 World Cup team of Holland. By then I had thought the idea through, carrying on where I had left off with Ajax, and preparing the Dutch team to try and play the new game.

The basis of pressing football is that attacking from the first moment is the priority. I have never liked defensive football and always wanted to attack. But to attack you need the ball, and if the opposition has the ball you must first win the ball from them. So thinking like this we did everything we could to obtain possession of the ball.

What is different about pressing football is that we did not fall back on our goal to defend when we lost possession. We tried to win the ball in all three lines of our team: in attack, in midfield and in defence. This is part of what was new: that when opposing defenders had the ball we tried to get it back from them without falling back on our goal to defend. *We pressed forward looking for the chance to win the ball back.*

Once we have got the ball then we can impose our attacking style of play on our opponents. We had to organise our game so that in the moment we lost possession of the ball, we did everything, even in the enemy's own defensive third of the field, to win the ball back.

Of course there are times when you are playing against a very good team, that they impose their style of play on you. You must accept that, and in those circumstances you have to drop back, but even then, you must first make the attempt to win the ball back before they can mount an attack.

So if we are forced to defend by a very good opponent then we have to adapt ourselves to that situation and defend.

But I do not want to defend unless I am forced to and so we organised our team to press forward for the ball and try to win the ball back in our opponent's half.

So pressing for the ball in our opponent's half is directly the opposite of *catenaccio*. In the Italian system, at the instant your team loses possession of the ball, everyone falls back towards your own goal with the maximum number of players in your own penalty area. From there, the *catenaccio* teams wait until the opposition makes a mistake and loses the ball, and this is followed by a quick counter-attack. That is a way of playing without taking any risks.

In pressing football you are taking a lot of risks because we actually throw players forward (see Diagram 21) at the moment when the opponents have won the ball. We are not going back into our penalty area to defend: we are not even going back into our own half of the field. When we have lost the ball we even press forward on their goalkeeper.

In Diagram 21, to give an example, the opposing right back has intercepted a pass and in that moment I want all my players to react positively. They are all instructed

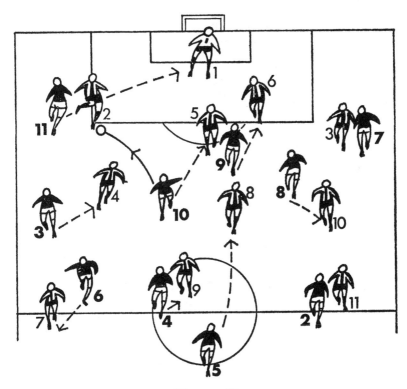

Diagram 21

to pick up the man closest to them, so that our left winger 11,goes on to mark the enemy goalkeeper to prevent a pass back to him. Everyone else takes up their new "pressing" positions on their closest opponent as indicated.

In general I want every opposing player marked in such a way that if a pass is made to him, then one of my players who is marking him can intercept the ball and thus allow us to start attacking once more.

If my centre forward loses the ball in a duel with his opponent, then I want the centre forward to go on and mark the *libero* or free back. Now the wingers mark the full backs, and the closest midfield player attacks the man with the ball—the enemy centre half—to put him under pressure and make him pass. Meanwhile every player that the centre half can pass to, has to be marked, and because we have thrown forward one of our midfield players to attack the enemy centre back in possession, then I have to reorganise the middle line.

The opposition will now have one midfield player free if my midfield men each mark one of their opposite numbers. So I solve this by sending forward my free man (*libero*) from the back line to mark the midfield opponent who is free. This is where I am taking the first risk.

It is very difficult to organise from a coaching viewpoint because football is always changing. First you are attacking and then you lose the ball. Then you are forced to defend and suddenly winning the ball back. The game changes constantly and this makes the organisation very difficult. Every individual player has to react to every new situation, first when attacking they have to get free, and then in the moment that we lose the ball they have to pick up and mark the nearest opponent, while my closest player to the man with the ball, attacks him and tries to dispossess him or force him to make a pass.

So in my philosophy, from the first moment that you lose the ball, the priority is to win it back. That is pressing football.

It is taking a big risk because not only do we commit our free back into midfield and leave our defence without an extra man to cover, but we take a risk because if just one man fails to pick up and mark an opponent that the man with the ball can pass to, then the opposition are invited to attack and the way is open for them.

For this reason you must have eleven intelligent and adaptable players, for we even ask the goalkeeper to move up to a position just outside his penalty area so that he can become the temporary *libero* and sprint out to kick the ball away if a long pass is made.

If only one of my players fails to do his job properly then we can get into trouble because automatically the opposition have a free player to whom they can pass. If this happens then the other players are running a lot to do their new tasks. The rest of my players are using a lot of energy while a good opponent finds the unmarked man with a pass, and all we have done is expended some of our precious energy to no purpose.

To organise this pressing football I started by talking to the players and explaining what I wanted when we lost the ball. I began with this systematic pressing football in my last year with Ajax, but I got even better results with this playing system when I introduced it to the players in Holland's national team in 1974.

It worked better with Holland because I had more good players to choose from and just to mention one man I had never had at my disposal before, Wim Jansen of Feyenoord proved himself to be very good at this kind of game.

You need really good players for pressing football, and if you do not have players of quality then you cannot play it.

To play pressing football you need intelligent players who know the game, who understand what football is about. In addition you also need two or preferably three players of what I call the "leader" type.

If you try to play this kind of game without the necessary players of quality and the leader types, then it is too difficult to play and too risky. If you do try it will be suicide.

A leader type of player is a really great player with most of the qualities demanded by modern football and something extra. He must be very skilled himself but also very intelligent and what makes him a leader type, is that while he can read the game and decide what he must do himself, he is so good that even in the fastest moving game, he still has time to spare to call to other players and tell them what they must do, who they must mark when we have lost the ball, and then, when we gain possession again, he can also prompt his colleagues and tell them where to go and what to do.

It is very difficult for the players because in addition to skill and intelligence, they also need one hundred per cent physical fitness so they can run for the whole game. Only in these conditions will they be able to keep pressing all the time, in all three lines of the team, and be adaptable enough to make it a successful system against teams that play to different formations and with different systems.

After explaining to each of the players what I wanted we began working at it in a small sided game with a goalkeeper and four outfield players on each side. Later this can be extended to six v. six and seven v. seven, but as a starting point, five against five is the maximum that I think is practical, for the coach has to try to pass instructions to the players all the time.

The basic idea of course is to score goals and ten minutes for each set of ten players will be quite enough to begin with. If necessary, because the exact numbers of players are not available then the four outfield players of one side can be changed after five minutes, and the first set of four players to go off can come back on again to replace the other four players who started the practice after a further five minutes. This would use two goalkeepers and twelve outfield players. If there are odd numbers of players then the players can come off and go on in rotation.

The coach should not increase the number of players beyond four and a goalkeeper against another five until the players have begun to get the idea of what is required of them, for the coach will find it impossible to prompt so many players to take the action he requires unless they have started to think about the game in the right way.

The team with the ball has to concentrate first on keeping possession, then on building an attack that leads to a shooting position, but above all, they must try not to give the ball away.

The other team that is defending (because they do not have the ball) has to do three things:

1. put pressure on the player with the ball
2. tight-mark the remaining players
3. have their goalkeeper in an advanced position, ready to come out still further if required.

As possession of the ball switches from one team to the other, each individual player must react. This is where the coach has to work hardest, spotting those that are slow to react. The essential point is that to cut down the amount of running that each player has to do, every man picks up the opponent closest to him, while the closest man to the ball challenges for possession.

Simply marking an opponent is not enough. We do not want to win the ball with sliding tackles for example. We want to intercept passes so that we can use the ball to mount an attack. Therefore the marking must be done in such a way that each player cuts out the passing angle available to the man he is marking and is in a position to intercept the ball if a pass is made to his man as described in Diagram 22.

Diagram 22

In the moment that the defending teams win the ball, the opponents have to do everything possible to get the ball back by organisation. So each man is running either to prevent the man with the ball from playing with it or making progress on his own, and trying to dispossess him, while the other players mark the men who might receive a pass.

This is very hard to do, because each player must look, think and respond like lightning, in the moment that the ball is lost. Each player must have stamina and make the right decisions for if two men go for the man with the ball for example, then somewhere there is a free opponent who can take a pass.

Thus if one man makes a mistake, then you are vulnerable. You need the ball and are pressing upfield to get it and mark everyone. But one man making the wrong decision can ruin everything. That is another risk.

When first introducing this type of training, with the coach looking everywhere for mistakes and calling to the players what to do and who to mark, then ten minutes will be quite enough. Ten minutes will be enough also at the start of the season when the players are not yet fully fit.

In my experience the players will be difficult to manage. In a squad of 15 to 20 players there are always two or three who want to play their own way.

Some players do not have the necessary mentality to change their way of playing. In them, the necessary mental strength is lacking. So you have to sort out those who can play this way or adapt themselves to the system, and this takes time.

The small sided game, a goalkeeper plus four players against five, gives them the general idea, and the coach can help. But even in this small game it requires a lot of energy to run almost constantly for ten minutes. Every player has to be on the move, virtually the whole time.

Physically it is easier than the strict, man for man marking game played by many other teams. That is more

demanding physically at some times but easier because each player knows who he must mark all the
time!

In that game, perhaps played best today in West Germany, the right back for example can move up to attack.
The opposing left winger knows that he should try to get
back and mark the right back and challenge him if he
gets the ball. But if the winger does not do this and the
attack breaks down, then the right back might have to
run as much as 60 yards very quickly to pick up his man
as in Diagram 23. Here we have a pass from the centre
forward 9, intended for the right back [2], intercepted by
the defending *libero*. Now the right back must sprint back
half the length of the pitch to mark his man.

Diagram 23

In pressing football, it would be our right midfield player who drops back to mark the enemy left winger, while the right back 2 may have to challenge the *libero* and lock him up so that he cannot pass, and put pressure on him to try to win the ball back. Alternatively, if a colleague is closer to the man now in possession then the right back would only have to pick up the enemy left midfield for example (his closest opponent) and would not have so far to run.

If it can be easier physically to play pressing football, it is certainly more difficult mentally, for each player must look and think. And if only one player makes the wrong decision then there is a risk again, because there will be a free man who can receive a pass.

So you are asking the players to mark the opponent who happens to be in the zone in which they find themselves temporarily and thus cover the shortest possible distance. One player (the closest) must attack the man with the ball while the others pick up the closest man to them. But as I have said before, if one man is looking for the wrong player then someone is free to receive a pass, and you are vulnerable. There is the risk.

To play pressing football you have to prepare the players physically, but you also have to prepare them for it mentally, because I have found that there are always some who do not like it.

Of course, being practical we have to play for a good result, and if we find ourselves a goal ahead we change our tactics a little. We still press the opposition by challenging the man with the ball and marking those closest to us, but we do not press forward. All our players now get goal-side of the ball, and if we let them come towards us, we always give them very little space in which to play. Challenging for the ball and tight-marking (to intercept) we let them come, but they are coming with a risk, because when we win the ball we throw everyone forward again.

If it is necessary, when for example your opponent is so strong, then we have to defend, but I want to contain the enemy attacks in midfield. We can go back a little, but whenever possible I want my players out of our defensive third of the pitch. The last thing I want is to see my players in our own penalty area, but of course against a very strong opponent we are sometimes forced back. Even then, however, I want everyone out into an attacking posture whenever we regain the ball. We only play in our own third of the pitch when there is no alternative. Because our opponent is very strong.

Many people think that my team is playing with an offside trap, but this is not so. Our opponents are often caught offside, but this is not through design. It happens sometimes because our free back presses forward to mark an opposing midfield player, but mostly it happens because my players are under orders not to fall back into our defensive third of the pitch unless absolutely vital, and when we have to do it, we get out as quickly as possible to press forward whenever we can.

If you are going to try and play pressing football, then as I have found, you have to work hard to change the style of play of the players. But if you are with a team like Ajax, and even more particularly with a club like CF Barcelona with their long history and standing, they inevitably want success. So you have to make the change more slowly, because it is always difficult to find and develop the players who can play pressing football.

In my first two years with Barcelona the players were awful. They had not the least idea what I wanted from them. We were especially bad in midfield and I had to recognise that we simply didn't have the players for it. But in the 1976–77 season, the first season of my second period with the club, they improved a lot, and they did rather well.

In midfield particularly you must have very good players. They must be technically very good and also very intelligent as well as being superbly prepared physically.

Johan Cruyff and Johan Neeskens were ideal for these roles. I do not need to say anything about Cruyff's technical qualities, but he was in addition one of the vital leader types, always giving advice to his colleagues, organising and re-organising. Neeskens had different qualities and was a powerful man. Together they played extremely well.

In organising pressing football it is very difficult. In the physical sense alone you have to prepare them more thoroughly than most other teams. In games the players must be able to run like dogs because you cannot play pressing football without that.

You can play football without maximum physical preparation, as many teams do, if you play like the Italians—waiting in defence until the opposition loses the ball, only attacking when you get the ball, playing a waiting game. My teams could always have played that style of football very easily, for intelligent covering in defence is the most important factor in the Italian game, and that is relatively easy to organise.

However, I have always believed that real football is attacking football, and the pressing game is based on attack for the whole ninety minutes. Wherever we lose the ball, even close to the enemy goal, I want my players to press forward to get it back, and they have to do it for ninety minutes. So physical preparation is the first thing. Without that you cannot play pressing football.

Technically there is a problem now as I explained earlier. It is clear that more and more of the players, say twenty years old now, have not developed their technique naturally by playing in the streets when young. So I am confronted by a lot of players who are lacking something in the technical sense; they are not fully equipped to play my kind of football. Most good players can control the ball and pass accurately if they are given time, but there are not so many who can demonstrate their skills when under pressure from an opponent who does not give them time.

Pressing football is perhaps the most difficult way of playing, because it demands so much from the players: top condition, superb technique, and a high degree of intelligence. The players have to change position very quickly in attack, and then when we lose the ball they have to take up pressing positions on individual opponents. The whole system breaks down very easily if one or two players are not doing their job properly and so we are playing with a lot of risk, and that puts a different kind of pressure on the players. If one man makes a mistake it can cost us a goal.

With my team looking for the ball all the time when the opponent is in possession, the back four have to press forward to the halfway line. That is also where I want the back four when the opposing goalkeeper has the ball and is going to try to start an attack with good distribution. But my free back has many considerations, and must be very intelligent and make decisions quickly. He has to look and think continuously, often waiting until the last moment. Sometimes I want my free back to move up to leave opponents offside. But at another moment he has to go back and cover; and then in another situation, the free back has to advance into midfield to pick up a free opponent. So pressing football makes great demands on the free back.

It is also new and difficult for the full backs. If as a

result of our pressing, we regain possession then I want my back four on the halfway line again, pushing forward. The full backs usually had to mark their wingers in the old system they were accustomed to, but if for example we are attacking, and a centre is going to come over from the left wing, then I want my right back up in support of the attack. The right back has to be well positioned to pick up a half clearance, or even to go forward and shoot or cross the ball if a pass is made to him.

In the moment that our attacks break down and the ball is pushed out of the enemy penalty area I don't want the man with the ball to be allowed to play quietly and with confidence. Given the chance his colleagues will come out looking for passes, and if we give the man on the ball any time at all then he can make a good pass.

It is in the moment that our attack breaks down that we are very vulnerable to a good, quick counter-attack, because we have thrown many of our players forward. When we were attacking we tried to create space, and in the moment we lose the ball that space is still there and an opponent who acts quickly can make use of that space we created, because for a few moments it is still there.

In that moment when our attacks break down we are very vulnerable because we have pushed one or two of our back four players forward. Now as I have said, in pressing football, our free back has to go forward into midfield to pick up the enemy's extra player there. So we are very open in the moment that we lose the ball.

This is where the lack of technique developed as boys comes out, because some of our players in attack make bad passes. As a result of one poor pass we lose possession and the enemy catches us at that moment when we are pressing forward and we are very vulnerable to a quick counter-attack.

With Barcelona this was my biggest problem for three years and it arises, not because of a lack of intelligence, but because of a lack of skill. I had too many players who were not skilful enough to make good passes in all situations and under pressure from opponents. In their own time they could have done it, but in the modern game, time is limited by tight-marking and quick tackling, and the lack of skill leads to passes going astray and we lose possession of the ball.

With Ajax at their peak this was not a problem. One of the greatest gifts about Ajax in the time of their biggest successes was that in terms of pure skill they were excellent. The Ajax players, say in the year before Cruyff left for Barcelona were really top class, and they had no problems in terms of skill and giving the ball away because of poor technique.

But with Barcelona I had problems in this sphere, because from the 15 best players I had 10 who had problems in reproducing their skills under pressure. They are the products of modern youth and didn't develop their skill to the necessary high degree when they were boys.

Cruyff had no problems and though Neeskens is not a great technical player he can make simple passes well. Neeskens also has a lot of other skills and qualities which add to the team's effect.

I worked a lot on this inability to make accurate passes starting with our goalkeeper and working the ball up to the halfway line, which is what you might call the constructing part of the game. The aim was to improve the quality of passing so that we did not give the ball away in our own half, because to do that can be disastrous, almost an invitation to the opposition to break through and score a goal.

In an attempt to improve the passing qualities of the players I put on a lot of small sided games in limited areas.

Five v. three; five v. four and then five v. five as the players got fitter at the start of the season. In these small sided games there is a lot of movement and a lot of passing and the conditions are almost like a match because there is opposition. To some degree this helps the players improve their skill.

Generally I think that one of the biggest problems for the future of the game can only be overcome if we start working on the development of skills and passing qualities at a very early age. Even beginning with six-year-old boys. The game is paying the penalty now because the current generation of players do not have a fully developed range of skills.

This was clear to me, even with a top club like Barcelona, and I cannot give the players the required level of skill. It is too late for that. I can get them to move around intelligently in attack, and I can improve the players in terms of their overall view of the game, getting them to look and think. But I do not see the technical qualities we need from a player who is 18 or 19 years old. Maybe if I worked only with one player for one hour or ninety minutes every day then it might be possible to bring players up to the level of skill required. But I cannot afford to spend that amount of time with one player because I must devote my attention to so many players. At top level with a big club you have to work for results or you find yourself out of a job.

There is no easy answer to this lack of individual technique. Not many young teenagers will give up the time to spend two hours a day working on technique, even if the clubs were to organise it.

Some clubs I know are beginning to work with nine- and ten-year-olds, working to improve their skills under pressure. But they are training only once or twice a week and you cannot compare that with previous generations who spent three hours or more *every day* playing in the streets or open fields.

If anyone wants to judge pressing football, or to get an idea of what it could be like then I suggest they watch films of Holland's games in the 1974 World Cup. This was the team with which my conception of the game was carried out almost ideally. I had a lot of success with this team because all the players were excellent in terms of technique. Most of them were also very intelligent and understood what I wanted from them quite easily.

In addition, I had three leader type of players in the squad and they were prompting the other players in the team organisation. These leader types are very difficult to find because this kind of player is constantly looking around and has good pictures of the situation in his mind all the time, and on top of that they also have imagination.

Technically the squad of Dutch players were very good, excellent in fact. The biggest problem with them was the physical preparation in quite a short time, but that went very well too, with everyone working very hard.

I do not think that the game will ever see football of such high quality again.

But fortunately there are films of their games so that if my prediction is true then future generations can see what pressing football was really like. I tried it with Barcelona and believe in pressing football so much that I will continue working with that as my aim whatever. But with Barcelona the players were not of the same quality in the technical sense so in this aspect of the game I always had a problem.

I have said already that if three or two or even one man is not doing what he should in the pressing game then we have problems. And with Barcelona we had real problems when Cruyff was not able to play for some reason, because he was our most important leader type.

Developing the constant movement that is necessary for pressing football is the problem, because for the players this conception is new. Holland played it very well and Ajax in my last year with them also played very well, even though it was never fully developed with them as an overall system.

If you want to see the best football today, and see it live with your own eyes then I think West Germany is the place to go. But they don't have the conception of pressing football even though in some ways it might look the same.

The Germans have a different conception of the game which is based on strict man-for-man marking. I have seen their club teams training and in training games based on four v. four for example, the players always stay on the same man.

I want my players to save their energy by picking up the opponent who is closest to them in the moment that we lose the ball. This is a combination between man-to-man marking and the old zonal system of defence: picking up the man who is in your immediate zone at any given moment.

Coaching attacking play is not easy either. But in this I have had more success. The players must have the intelligence to move into space to get away from tight-marking opponents. I try to coach them, giving them ideas, telling them where to go in small sided games, say five v. five. Sometimes I talk to them first about moving off the ball, and show them diagrams on a blackboard immediately before we go out to work on the training ground.

It is not a problem to get a full back to move upfield and join his attacking colleagues. This is because every player who really likes football loves to attack, and above all he likes scoring goals. The problem is that once he has got attacking ideas, you have to get him to accept his responsibilities in defence, and only move upfield when there is space, not simply because he enjoys it.

The first priority for a full back is to eliminate the man he is marking, usually the opposing winger. If the back can play his opponent out of the game, then he can attack. But if the full back is not eliminating his man; if the opponent is a very good player and dangerous, then the only thing for a full back to do is to defend and try to contain his man.

I have found that once I begin to give attacking ideas to a defender, he tends to start ignoring his defensive responsibilities, and then I have to restrain him.

A sense of responsibility is very important in modern football, particularly in a team that encourages back four players to attack. In the modern game, there is a lot of positional changing going on but defenders must put defence first when necessary.

I use some practices that encourage the full backs to go forward and, at the same time, the midfield player on that flank has to hold back and temporarily mark the opposing winger. But it is difficult to coach even these two players in how to react when our move breaks down because no two counter-attacks are ever the same exactly. We can recreate very roughly what might happen and a situation that must be covered, but this still leaves the players with a lot of responsibility to use their intelligence and make decisions.

I have other practices that we use in small sided games at first, because in small groups there are fewer players, and therefore it is easier for the players to get "pictures" of the situation I am trying to coach, and get them clear in their minds. But we always meet the same problems: the players want to do too much, they want to attack and score a goal.

This mentality goes right through the team, and the lack of a sense of responsibility brings problems in matches. An attacking midfield player by nature does not want to cover for a full back, even temporarily. Such players do not like being in the back four—they want to attack. So you have to find the right balance.

It is a lot of work and cannot be achieved in one month or even two. It takes years to give the players the right mentality and a sense of responsibility if they do not have it naturally.

I have found that in a squad of 20 players, roughly half of them will have a natural sense of responsibility, but the other half will be very difficult to deal with.

I find that you have to talk with the players, instructing them all the time, but you also have to work on the training ground in practical situations. But because of the possibilities open to an attacking team and the fact that no two balls ever come exactly the same, you can only coach past situations. The next game will bring new attacks and new problems, and the players must look and think and make decisions. Because every attack is different you can only give them ideas and force them to think for themselves.

Only having worked in two countries, I don't know how it is elsewhere, but in general I have found that the Spanish players are very lazy. They do not want to think. You cannot play football without looking and thinking and talking. I had to fight with the Barcelona players all the time.

A coach can only give his players rough ideas and I had to fight with the players and say "Look, this is only a possibility for the game tomorrow. So you must look and think and talk." You have to work very hard with them, instructing them and constantly pushing the players.

Spanish players in general have their own way of playing and never try to boss each other by talking. I have to
press them to shout advice to each other and never cease
to demand that they think and talk to each other.

TO PLAY FOOTBALL THE OTHER WAY—WITHOUT YOUR
EYES IN YOUR MOUTH, IS A DESERT!

Modern football has changed the game a lot, making
new demands on the players, but pressing football asks
so much more. Each player must force his team-mate to
look and think and do things. The leader type of player
does this naturally, talking to his colleagues during the
game, but I want all the players to talk to each other, to
look and think and act. Because there is always at least
one player who forgets things and does not react to a
given situation, his closest colleagues who can see the
situation, must "live it" for him, and force the forgetful
player to react by shouting. If the players do not develop
this way then they will never improve.

At this particular period in time we are developing this
kind of thinking and playing, because in football we can
improve a lot.We are nowhere near the limit of the players'
possibilities.

If you want to play good football, then I think the
pressing game is best. It is the best kind of football for
the spectators, and I think it will become the only way of
playing in the future.

People, and the club supporters in particular, are asking
more and more of the professional players. In my experience, even at a top club like Barcelona, the players do not
have a professional mentality. They still want to take the
line of least resistance.

I am coaching the players to play pressing football, and
if this is to be achieved, you always have to go to the
extreme limits of your powers. So I have to be constantly
pushing them and forcing them.

A good professional who is paid very well has to be intelligent and skilful, perfectly prepared physically, and also has to be an ambitious player. Without ambition, players in the modern game will get nowhere. Certainly they will not be able to play pressing football.

But many of the Barcelona players (and they are not alone) still do not have the necessary ambition. They still have the old idea that playing football for a living is a well paid hobby!

What we need is a player whose hobby is football, but is also a hard worker. If football is not the player's hobby, if he does not love the game, then he is only a skilled worker like a factory hand. If the players do not have a real feeling for the game then they will never be top class today.

In the old game, the players could afford to show off their skill and think only a little. But modern football has changed all that and brought a whole new set of problems. The old days are over. Past. Gone for ever.

At Barcelona I had an excellent player called Rexach. He had marvellous skills, perhaps even more skilful than Cruyff. But Rexach wasn't a power in the team, and he wasn't ambitious, and I couldn't improve him. I couldn't make him change his basic approach to the game.

Repeatedly I used to say to Rexach . . . "Listen my boy. Five years ago you had no problems and were a star player. But today the opposition will not let you play as you did then and you must adapt yourself to the needs of the modern game and try to play the kind of football I want. The enemy doesn't want you to play because you are too skilful and because you could dominate the game they are afraid of you. So they have created a new style of play that is designed to prevent stars like you from dominating with your skill. So you have to change because unless you do, you will never escape from their tight-marking, quick tackling and good covering".

The top player today must be able to escape from the net the enemy tries to drape around him. Only then can he begin to play, to show his skill. Rexach is very skilful, beautiful to watch on the ball, and he has the ability to play the ball with superb accuracy. I love to watch him in action, but he cannot change.

Cruyff was able to change, looking for ways to escape and adapting himself.

Rexach on the other hand cannot do it, and then after a game he looks for excuses, trying to blame others. I really sympathise with him, because he is typical of many players who are losing out in modern football. He is losing out because he cannot adapt his style of play so that he can still use his skills. He cannot develop the new skills, or use his skills in the new way in order to maintain his position as a star.

I began to develop pressing football with Ajax, though in a slightly different way. I began with the extra mobility of the play and players in attacking situations.

Then later I thought to myself, everything is going so well when we are able to attack. We have players with a lot of attacking skills so that if we can dominate the game and keep possession of the ball we can always win. But to attack we must have the ball, and so I began to think about situations when we lost the ball and tried to develop it. But at that time I had only got the germ of an idea, a notion, but I hadn't thought it out to its ultimate. By 1974 I had my new conception of the game, my ideas were fully developed. And with the whole of Holland to choose from I had at my disposal a squad of players with all the skills, the right mentality and the willingness to work at my ideas and make them pay.

I am sure the fans liked the play of Holland in the 1974

World Cup. This is my idea of the modern game as it could be. I shall keep trying to reproduce pressing football for I believe it to be the game of the future. But I doubt if I will ever have a squad of players again who can play it so well.

7/ Coaching Ball Skills for Young Players

by **Frank Blunstone**

Frank Blunstone was born at Crewe on 17th October 1934 and on leaving school joined the ground staff of Crewe Alexandra as an inside left. Transferred to Chelsea in 1953 he was converted into a left winger and played for the England Youth team, the Under 23 side and the full England XI.

He began his coaching career at Chelsea between 1965 and 1969 before spending four years as manager of Brentford.

In 1973 Blunstone moved to Manchester United where he coached the Youth team and helped many players who were later to become first team players.

Under Tommy Docherty, he later became assistant manager at Manchester United and in 1977 moved with Docherty to Derby County.

In recent years, young players have not played soccer for hours on end in street games or various open spaces, as their predecessors did. Many generations of players were brought up using a tennis ball in scratch games and playing for hours, almost every day, developed their skills naturally. Only in parts of the world that are still very largely undeveloped do the youngsters still play with the ball for long periods. Elsewhere, the resultant drop in levels of technique can never be made up, but attempts must be made to improve the basic skills of players while they are still relatively young.

Frank Blunstone has drawn on his experience in this chapter, from the period spent coaching players between 15 and 18 years at Manchester United. Other professional clubs all over Europe make similar efforts with the best young players they can find.

In the advanced societies of Europe and North America, technical deficiencies must be made up before the players reach first team level when the coaches are too much involved with other things to give specialised coaching to one player.

Although Frank Blunstone's practices were designed for young professionals in their middle teens, time spent practising the various skills described will be of immense value to boys and teenagers everywhere. There is no age at which it is too early to get young players to practise their skills, and even the best young players tend to be very good only with their best foot. From Sofia to Seattle, youngsters will benefit from skill practices, even if it is only to improve their weaker foot, for time spent perfecting their technique will stand them in good stead for the rest of their playing lives.

RECEIVING THE BALL WITH THE RIGHT FOOT, THE LEFT FOOT AND THE CHEST

Basic Technique: the part of the body to be used should move towards the oncoming ball, but at the moment of contact, the foot or the chest should be withdrawn in order to take the pace off the ball. It is important that the muscles should be as relaxed as possible. The player should move into the flight of the ball and keep his eyes on it while playing it.

INSIDE OF THE FOOT

When trapping with the inside of the foot, a trapping angle is made by the foot and ankle to be used—and the ground. To kill the ball and leave it nicely placed to be played again, the force of impact as the ball makes contact with the foot is cushioned by relaxing the trapping leg and withdrawing it.

OUTSIDE OF THE FOOT

This trap is only used when a player wishes to receive the ball and move off with it in another direction, for example with a ball coming from the player's right, the ball can be trapped with the outside of the left foot and moved to the left.

The trap is made across the standing leg with the trapping leg moved across the body before the ball arrives. The ball is received with the trapping foot turned outwards, forming a trapping angle between the ground and the ankle and the outside of the trapping foot. As the outside of the foot makes contact with the ball, the trapping leg is swept across the body, bringing the ball with it.

RECEIVING THE BALL WITH THE CHEST

The player should get in line with the flight of the ball with his chest relaxed, knees slightly bent and both arms extended at the sides to help retain balance, and avoid handling the ball. On impact the chest is withdrawn so that the ball drops down nicely at the feet of the player.

EXERCISES TO PRACTISE RECEIVING THE BALL
Players practise in groups of three, formed in triangles
about twenty yards apart, as in Diagram 24. Player A

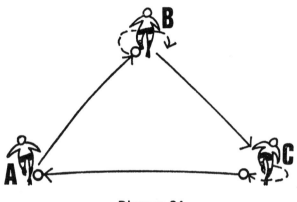

Diagram 24

passes to B who receives the ball with the inside or outside
of the right foot or the left foot as instructed by the
coach. Player B receiving the ball controls it and makes a
three-quarter turn before passing to player C who repeats
and passes on to A and so on.

Use both high and low passes.

To practise receiving the ball with the chest the players
should be disposed in triangles again with one ball between three as in Diagram 24. This time player A gives
player B a high ball to receive on his chest and when B
has controlled it, he passes on another high ball for player
C to control with his chest before passing on to player A,
and repeat.

Should the players not be skilled enough to kick a ball
so that it can be controlled with the chest they should
serve the ball to each other by throwing it with the hands.

Once the players have acquired a certain degree of skill at controlling the ball with the chest, a challenge should be added. The triangles can now be made smaller with the players about ten yards apart. As player A serves the ball for B to control it with his chest, player C sprints to challenge B who must control the ball with his chest and return an accurate pass to player A. Now the players can have five to ten attempts to control the ball each, before they change places so that everyone gets a turn in each role.

Another practice for receiving the ball is described in Diagram 25 with the players in pairs and one ball between

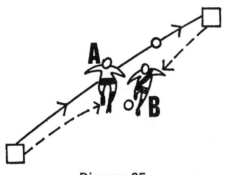

Diagram 25

two. The players should be twenty to twenty-five yards apart and player A begins by passing to player B who must control the ball as laid down by the coach, for example by controlling the ball with the outside of the right foot. As soon as player A has made his pass he sprints to challenge player B who, having controlled the ball, now tries to dribble past player A.

Repeat with B passing to A, and vary the type of serve by using both high and low passes.

Another practice requires more balls so that each player has one ball to himself. Several players can have a ball each in a large area and they should be instructed to keep the ball up in the air using their feet only. At a signal from the coach, each player has to kick his ball high into the air above him and then trap the falling ball as laid down by the coach. For example, first with the outside of the left foot, then the second time with the outside of the right foot and so on.

When the players are confident with the ball a feint movement can be introduced with the players pretending to move off in one direction, but then controlling the ball to move away in another direction.

As a variation, once the ball has been kept up in the air with several touches of the feet only, the coach can instruct the players to kick their ball high in the air and then receive the ball with their chests.

Another simple skill practice is described in Diagram 26. Six to twelve players line up as indicated, facing each

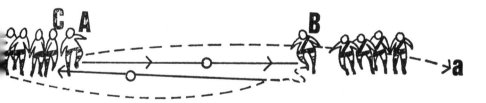

Diagram 26

other about twenty to twenty-five yards apart. Using both high and low passes according to instructions from the coach, player A begins by playing the ball to B who controls the ball as laid down by the coach, for example by feinting to move right, then coming back to control the ball with the outside of the left foot. Having controlled the ball, B then passes as instructed to player C for him to control the ball, while players A and B run to the end of the opposite rows.

By now the players should be skilled enough to test themselves against live opposition and a good practice for this is described in Diagram 27. Players A and D should be fifty to sixty yards apart, with B and C halfway

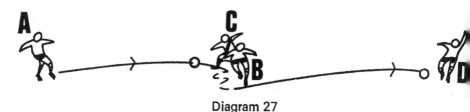

Diagram 27

between them. According to the instructions of the coach, which should be varied from time to time, player A gives the suggested type pass to player B who must control the ball and, at the same time, evade the challenge of player C. The challenge of player C must be unrestricted except that he must not commit a foul, while player B has to pass to player D in spite of the opposition of player C.

Players B and C now change roles with B challenging C while player D serves as instructed.

After players B and C have each received five or ten passes they should change places with A and D, and go on repeating.

In this way, having practised their skills without opposition, they are now asked to reproduce their skills in conditions that are something like a match with live opposition.

Taking this line of thinking a step further the coach can now set up a small game two v. two and a goalkeeper with A and B attacking and trying to score against the goalkeeper and the two defenders C and D.

The coach should stand on or about the halfway line and start the practice by passing to either player A or player B as they move into a good position. In the example given in Diagram 28 players A and B have made a cross-over run and with one defender following player A, player B is comparatively free to receive a pass from the coach. This initial pass can be varied from a low ball to be received by the feet or by a high ball to be taken on the chest.

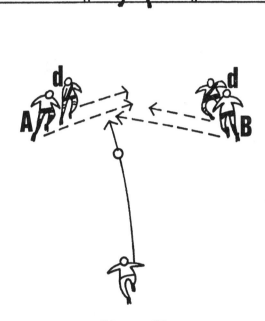

Diagram 28

The attacking players A and B now have a match-like situation in which they must use all their skills and try by feints and dummy runs to get unmarked, break through and score. All this time of course the two defenders are trying to mark A and B, challenging for the ball and feinting to tackle, while the attacking players must receive the ball and turn, then inter-pass or dribble past defenders and try everything they know to shoot and score. If a defender wins the ball he must dribble it to the coach.

GENERAL ADVICE ON THINGS THAT GO WRONG IN SKILL PRACTICES

(a) The muscles are too tense causing the ball to bounce off the foot too far.

(b) The part of the body receiving the ball moves to meet it too late and does not move far enough.

(c) The part of the body receiving the ball moves too early or too late to take the pace off the ball.

(d) The player takes his eye off the ball.

(e) The player reads the flight of the ball wrongly.

(f) Not enough weight is placed on the supporting leg when receiving high balls and the result is that the player hits the ball with part of the body-weight and the ball bounces away.

THINGS THAT MANY YOUNG PLAYERS FIND DIFFICULT

(a) They have difficulty mastering a given skill because of the very high speed at which they try to perform the practice.

(b) In my experience when coaching schoolboys and young professionals only a limited number could perform the techniques of receiving the ball with the outside of the foot and with the chest. This requires extra practice when young.

(c) The player anticipates the arrival of the ball either too late or too soon and fails to take the pace off the ball.

(d) The player takes his eye off the ball which results in making his move too late to take the pace off the ball and sometimes even missing the ball completely.

THE ART OF DRIBBLING
Basically there are two types of dribble:
1. The close dribble where the player is restricted due to close marking which limits his space, or where he does not have great acceleration and relies on feints to beat his man.
2. The running dribble where there is space for the player to gather speed and pass an opponent on pace alone.

DRIBBLING TECHNIQUE
Dribbling is a combination of guiding the ball, stopping and starting with it, turning on the spot, taking the ball round curves, changing direction and making feints. These skills form the basis of good dribbling technique.

The good dribbler always keeps the ball within comfortable playing distance with his body evenly balanced so that he can suddenly move off in any direction. He should try to throw his opponent off balance by pretending to move off in one direction while actually intending to move away in another direction. He achieves this objective by various movements of the body and his feet.

RUNNING AT AN OPPONENT
The ability to dribble at speed towards a retreating opponent and then beat him by increasing speed requires considerable practice and skill. Changing direction while moving at top speed is a difficult but important technique Such an opponent can be beaten in two ways:

1. By good ball control and the use of body feints, the good dribbler causes his opponent to move first one way, then the next, and finally render him incapable of making any challenge at all because he has completely lost his balance.
2. The dribbler feints to go one way, then accelerates in that same direction with the opponent having reacted to the feint, he has leaned that way, shifting his body-weight on to that foot and then the second movement in that direction catches the defender with his weight on what should be the tackling foot.

Dribbling Practices

(a) Several players with a ball each dribble the ball with a slow, economical movement in straight lines, curved lines, figures of eight or circles according to the instructions of the coach.
(b) As above but using right foot or left foot as coach instructs, and also according to the requirements of the coach, dribble by using the inside or the outside of the right foot or the inside or outside of the left foot.
(c) Sprint with the ball under close control and at a command (or whistle) from the coach, change direction.
(d) Players practise in pairs to offer a challenge. A sets off dribbling with the ball while player B chases him and according to the coach's command attempts to rob A of the ball from behind, approaching from the right side or left side of player A, as the coach has previously instructed.
(e) Two players face each other about twenty yards apart with player A in possession. A passes to B, then runs after the ball to challenge B, who tries to dribble past him. Repeat with B passing to player A

who is then given his chance to dribble round the opposition.

(f) As in (e) except that player C is added to form a triangle. A has the ball and attacks B, trying to dribble past him. If A is successful he passes to C for him to attack B, while if player B makes a successful tackle he now attacks C. Repeat.

(g) Six to ten players, stand in pairs behind each other, the first to be a dribbler trying to score against a live goalkeeper, the second to offer a challenge.

Starting well outside the penalty area, the coach passes the ball in any direction for the first pair, A the dribbler and B the defender to tackle. A has to use his body to screen the ball, but being closely challenged he must use a high degree of skill, feinting and weaving in order to turn on the ball and face his challenger, then dribble past him and score. If B (the challenger) wins the ball, then the two players immediately change roles with B trying to score. Repeat for the next pair and so on.

Obviously, some of the practices requires more skill than others and small boys and lesser skilled young amateurs should start with the easier practices until skilled enough to take on an opponent as in (g) above, with an added centre back who can provide even more opposition.

ADVICE ON THINGS THAT GO WRONG

1. The players legs are not bent so that the centre of gravity of the dribbler has not been lowered from the normal position.

2. Players try to make feints when moving too fast. The dribbler should start making feints in a standing position, then at a slow trot, and when moving at

top speed, slow down immediately before throwing a feint.

3. When dribbling, the player must watch not only the ball but also the behaviour of the opponent—and react accordingly.
4. The player allows the ball to run too far ahead of him.
5. After making a feint, the player is slow to change direction and accelerate quickly. Try the movements without a ball.
6. The feint is made too close to the opponent (and too late), or too far away from the challenger which gives him time to regain his balance and offer a successful challenge. Timing is of prime importance when feinting.

THINGS THAT YOUNG PLAYERS FIND MOST DIFFICULT

1. To keep the head up while controlling the ball, this alone makes it possible to watch his challenger and look around for colleagues that might be free and in a good position to receive a pass.
2. Dribble using all four outside surfaces of the two feet. Answer: more practice at the weakest skill, almost certainly the outside of the weaker foot.

THE PRACTICE OF PASSING SKILLS

Two distinctly separate types of pass can clearly be identified:

(a) Low passes—usually over short distances.
(b) Passes that are lofted into the air—usually over longer distances.

Full instep kick

Various surfaces of the foot can be used to make a

pass though the instep kick is the most natural and also the most widely used. The ball can be played short or long with the instep, and also both low and high, while it is the best kick for scoring goals.

Another clear advantage with the instep kick is that it can be carried out while travelling at full speed, without changing pace and without having to twist the foot around.

The technique is simple: the supporting leg should be around a foot's width away from the ball, foot pointing in the direction that the ball will travel, and the knee slightly bent.

The kicking leg swings back at the hip and knee joints, the hip straightening first as the kicking action develops, then on contact with the ball the knee joint becomes straight and the follow through is in a straight line with the leg in a straight line. The foot is also stretched as flat as possible on contact, and the ball is played with the arch of the foot.

Inside of the foot kick

High and low balls alike can be kicked accurately with the inside of the foot, making it one of the most used skills and therefore one of the most important to perfect.

To execute, the higher part of the body should be bent over the ball—depending on the intended flight path of the ball—and the arms extended for balance.

The supporting leg should have the toes pointing in the direction the ball is intended to travel, bent at the knee, ankle and hip. The kicking leg has the foot turned outwards at an angle of 90 degrees to the direction of play, toes tightened and the sole of the foot parallel to the ground with the ankle stiffened during the execution of the kick.

The area of contact with the ball is the whole of the

inside of the foot from the side of the big toe area, right down the foot including the ankle bone to the heel bone.

Inside of the instep kick

This kick enables a player to curve and lift the ball over the head of an opponent who may even be quite close. Here the supporting leg should be about two or three "foot widths" away from the ball and more bent than for the instep kick. The trunk should lean to the side over the supporting leg while the kicking leg should be slightly turned out at hip and ankle. The area of contact with the ball is the inside edge of the instep between the bottom of the toes and the ankle bone.

Kicking with the outside of the foot

This kick can be used to curve the ball as well, but can also be used for straight passes and is especially good for short disguised passes to the side.

The whole leg is used to give power to a sharp kick, but a quick flick of the ankle is all that is needed to push the ball out to the side. The upper body is bent slightly forward and also towards the side of the supporting leg. The supporting leg should be about two "foot widths" away from the ball, toes turned away from the direction that the ball will travel—towards the kicking leg. The kicking leg should be turned inwards and downwards and the ankle should be stiffened.

The area of contact is the whole of the outside of the foot from the bottom of the toes to the ankle bone.

The descriptions of the above kicks for passing are also entirely applicable to the section for shooting practices which follow passing.

Passing practices

Three players A, B and C form a triangle as in Diagram

29 with the coach instructing the players on which part of which foot they must try to receive and play the ball as he requires, according to their abilities.

Player C starts the practice by playing the ball in low for B to receive it and then player C immediately sprints to take up a new position as shown. Player B then controls the ball and passes low for A before sprinting around the back of player A (overlapping him) to take up his new position. Meanwhile A continues the passing practice by laying a nice ball into the path of player C in his new position who controls the ball and turns.

From there the players inter-pass between themselves as they return to their starting positions, again using the type of the pass ordered by the coach, and at regular intervals the positions of the three players should be switched around.

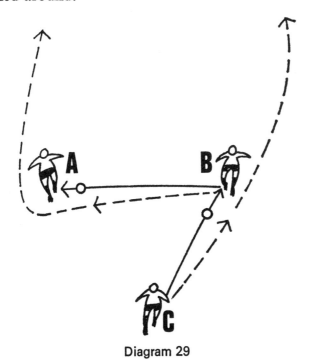

Diagram 29

As lesser, younger players improve, and as soon as the coach wishes with older players or young professionals, an element of opposition can be added to the practice described in the Diagram. Two defenders can be added, one on the back of player B and another on the back of player C. As each player receives a pass he will be challenged and must evade the defender before making his pass.

Again players A, B and C should frequently change positions with the defenders.

The markings of the pitch can be used for a good practice that will show the players how accurate their straight passes are, and also how much they are able to bend the ball when required.

All the touchlines can be used plus the goal line and halfway line, as well as the markings of the penalty area and goal area if there are enough players. There should be one ball between two players who position some twenty yards apart.

The coach should wander about amongst the pairs, commenting on their accuracy or lack of it, and generally giving advice to players who are not using the appropriate body movements required for each skill.

SUGGESTED PRACTICES
   (a) The man with the ball drives it hard and low for his partner to receive it in the manner prescribed by the coach, e.g. with the inside of the left foot.
   (b) The ball should be chipped up, and dropped for the partner to receive—with the chest or thigh for very skilled players, but perhaps any way they can for young players.
   (c) Bend the ball on either side of the line using the appropriate kick and using both high and low passes.
   (d) The players can inter-pass using two touches only.

It is important that the coach specifies which foot each skill should be practised with, remembering that not all players are skilled enough to chip and curve a ball with their weaker foot. Left-footed players should use that foot for the most difficult skills. Players receiving the ball should be under varied orders so that they improve their ability at receiving the ball with both the left and right foot, and with the inside and outside of each foot.

A good first time passing practice is to have the players (from six to twelve of them) split into two lines in single file, facing each other with the two front players some twenty yards apart.

The first player in one file begins the practice with a pass to the front player in the opposite file who runs towards the ball while the player who gave the first pass has run off at an angle. The player receiving the ball has to find the man who passed to him with a good ball and from there the player passes to the next player in the file that did not start the practice. The first two players now go to the back of the opposite lines while the practice continues with the next pair of players.

A more complicated passing practice is described in Diagram 30 which involves five players. Player E begins the practice with a pass to player A who sprints to meet the ball and lays it off first time for E who has come in support. Player A then turns away "looking for a through pass" and E plays the ball nicely ahead of A as he makes his run.

Player E now positions himself between A and B, while A collects the ball, then gives it to B who repeats the practice with player D coming to meet the ball before looking for a through pass, and then with the ball returned to C, he attempts to put player E away and then the practice continues to flow with A providing the ball and the support to player C to make his run, and so on.

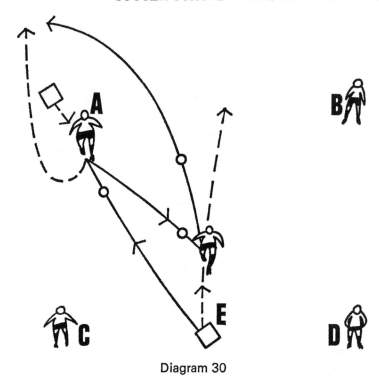

Diagram 30

ADVICE ON THINGS THAT GO WRONG

1. Particularly with very young players, failure to achieve accuracy over both long and short distances through lack of concentration.
2. Players take their eyes off the ball when actually striking it. This results in striking the wrong part of the ball or playing it with the wrong part of the foot. This is especially true when making lofted or bent passes.
3. The players do not adjust their body correctly in relation to the ball and passes go astray as a result.
4. In the group practices, players fail to make good angles for themselves in relation to the player who will give them the ball.
5. The ball is not played with the right amount of

weight behind it, thus making it difficult for the receiving player to catch it, let alone control it in the manner specified by the coach.

6. The timing of the pass is wrong, played too early or late for a colleague in movement with the result that the ball goes astray.

7. The players indicate their intentions by taking up the correct body stance too early.

THINGS THAT YOUNG PLAYERS FIND MOST DIFFICULT

1. Youngsters find it difficult to vary their passing, e.g. long and short passes; passes in front of and behind a colleague, and passes to feet and into space. Patience by the coach, hard work and encouragement will improve matters.

2. Strike the correct part of the ball when making lofted (chipped) passes or when trying to bend the ball

3. Free themselves when tightly marked by an opponent.

4. Bend the ball according to given circumstances, e.g. to bend the ball away from the goalkeeper when crossing high, and bending a ball into the stride of a colleague.

SHOOTING PRACTICE

Shots at goal are made with various parts of the foot, all dealt with under previous headings, but in many players the ability to shoot may be there, while the inclination to do so, is not.

Regular goalscorers are probably born, but a good coach can help other players to acquire the habit of shooting—with constant practice.

Shooting practices

Any number of players, though preferably between six and ten, divide themselves into two lines in Indian file about twenty yards apart, and twenty yards outside the penalty area, faced only by a goalkeeper.

The coach positions himself equidistant between the two lines of players, on the edge of the penalty area, and because of the longish range, players should use the instep kick for shooting.

The first player in the left hand file passes the ball to the coach—and then sprints towards goal hoping to score a tap in goal if the ball rebounds off the goalkeeper or comes back into play off the crossbar or a post. Meanwhile the coach lays off a first time pass with his left foot, for the first player in the right hand file to run onto and shoot right-footed. After the first effort on goal has been completed, the coach now receives a pass from the next player in the right hand file (who sprints ahead looking for the soft goal) while the coach lays off a good pass with his right foot for the next player in the left hand file to sprint forward and shoot with the full instep, and the practice continues with each pair of players re-joining their file after each attempt.

A more individual practice can be set up in several ways, all basically organised the same way. Four to six players line up in Indian file on the halfway line, each with a ball.

At the command from the coach the first player dribbles the ball forward, keeping it close but making five touches of the ball with the inside of the foot ordained by the coach. Immediately after the fifth touch the player shoots at goal with the instep . . . and repeat with the first player going to retrieve his ball before going to the end of the file to await his next turn.

The same practice can be carried out, making five touches of the ball with the outside of the foot, and of course the coach can instruct the players to use their strongest foot or their weaker one as he prefers.

Another alternative to this basic practice will really test the ball skills of the players. At the word from the coach, the first player flicks the ball up into the air, keeping the ball up for any number of touches as ordered by the coach, before lobbing the ball forward in the air. The player then sprints after his ball, sets himself up for a shot by controlling the ball with his chest and propelling it forward nicely, and then finishes with a shot.

Another practice will give the players the chance to improve their finishing at different types of shooting, as described in Diagram 31. Nine or twelve players are positioned at different angles to the goal in three groups of three or four. The coach will control the session by calling on the first player in each file by name when he is to set off, bearing in mind that the goalkeeper must have time to re-position himself.

Diagram 31

The coach should point out the best possible scoring chances from each angle of approach: the players in B file will probably be most successful with a full-blooded instep drive; players in file C will probably find that the goalkeeper covers the near-post shot, and their best chance is a curved ball, bent back into the far corner of the net, and players approaching from a narrower angle as in file A will have to concentrate on precision to a much more marked degree and probably their best chance will be to try and squeeze the ball past the goalkeeper, or under his body to score with a shot between the goalkeeper and the near post.

A shooting practice that requires observation of the goalkeeper as well as shooting skill can be set up by having two files of players, roughly at what used to be inside left and inside right in Indian file with the first players some thirty to thirty-five yards from goal. Each file is serviced by a ball from a server who should be changed frequently, positioned facing each file.

The player serving to the first man in the inside left file, lays the ball in while the shooting players run to meet the ball and can either shoot first time or take a touch to control the ball, as the coach instructs. After his shot each player returns to the end of the opposite file to shoot with either foot.

The coach supervises the practice and instructs the servers when to play the ball in, and the shooting players have always to look up as they approach the oncoming ball to note the reaction of the goalkeeper.

If the goalkeeper comes too much off his line as he tries to narrow the shooting angle, then the players should try to score by either lobbing the ball over him into the net or by chipping the ball with an instep kick, played with the inside of the foot.

Perhaps the volley is the most difficult shooting skill to

acquire for it has to be made first time, and hit when the ball is in the air. Power can be achieved in two ways, either by waiting until the ball is as near the ground as possible, and the player then has to lean away backwards, turning down the point of the toes, stretching out the ankle and keep it fixed in this position . . . this technique will cause the ball to dip late in flight. Alternatively, the ball can be struck at a higher point, but the higher the point at which the ball is struck, the less will the player be able to use a full leg swing, and he will have to lean away both backwards and sideways (away from the ball) as he swings his kicking leg . . . this technique allows the shot to be struck earlier and if the player leans well away from the ball it can be kept reasonably low.

A simple practice for this involves eight players, four to serve and four to shoot, and of course they should change places frequently.

Two serving players are positioned at the points on each side of the goal, where the goal-line meets the line of the penalty area. The shooting players are positioned at the opposite corners of the penalty area, so that the server plays his ball across goal.

To avoid chaos the coach should call out who is to shoot and order the serving players to get his ball across, and after say five attempts each, all eight players can move round in a clockwise direction so they all get a turn at serving (which is itself a skill practice), and all will get a chance to volley with both the right and left foot.

As a variation, the coach can instruct the shooting players to control the ball with their chest before volleying at goal.

Another good volleying practice involves the coach more directly. Six to eight players stand in line, parallel with the 18 yard line, some six to eight yards away from it. The players start with their backs to goal with the coach facing them with a supply of balls. After each attempt, the shooting player must return his ball to the coach before joining the end of the queue for another shot.

The coach faces the first player and lobs the ball over the player's head and he turns and sprints after the ball, allowing it to bounce once before hitting a full instep volley at goal.

A variation to this is to lob the ball up higher and instruct the players to hit the ball before it bounces, though this may be more difficult to achieve.

As the shooting ability of the players improves they should begin to observe the reactions of their particular opponent more and more, as they will need to do in match play. For this reason, shooting practices involving one v. one situations plus a goalkeeper should be created for shooting practices. A good one is to position forwards and defenders on the halfway line, with the forward having a start of three to five yards according to the estimate of their ability by the coach.

The forward has the ball at his feet, and at the signal from the coach, the forward sprints towards goal with the ball, chased hard by the defender. The forward must obviously be aware of the defender and take appropriate action by screening the ball, and also note the position and movements of the goalkeeper.

If the defender is getting close enough to tackle, a full blooded instep drive will probably have the best chance of scoring.

If the forward can get closer to goal he should concentrate more on precision and make his shot as accurate as possible.

If the goalkeeper comes too far out, the forward can make an attempt to lob the ball over his head and into the net.

Another good one v. one plus the goalkeeper practice

is to line up three or four attacking players on the half-way line, and an equal number of defenders positioned, first on the right hand corner of the penalty area, and later on the left, to try and prevent a shot at the goal-keeper.

The practice starts with the first forward, ball at his feet, setting off at a signal from the coach, to try and break through to score. As the forward moves so can the first defender. The forward tries to disguise his intentions, can pretend to try a lob, can feint, change direction and try to dribble. In effect he is through in a match-like situation with only one player to beat to get in a shot at goal.

Repeat with the second pair of forward-defenders, while the first two return to their files to wait for their next turn.

The coach plays a big part himself in the next practice, two v. two and a goalkeeper, inside the penalty area. Because the practice is quite exhausting, two further teams of two and two can be brought on at say, three minute intervals, thus involving twelve players in all.

The coach has the ball, positioned say on the penalty spot, while the two defenders are each detailed to tight-mark one attacking player. The attacking players fly around, trying everything they can to get free or at least be in a position where the coach can give them a good pass with which they can try to score first-time, or at least, screen the ball from their opponents and try to work a shooting position.

Clearly the attacking players must move around a lot, changing pace and direction very frequently and disguis-ing their intentions in a bid to get free. The attacking players may well benefit from a tip from the coach, that close to goal, a full leg-swing shot is often not necessary. Frequently it is enough to use the side of the foot, or even a toe-end stab to score a goal when close in.

This form of practice can be built up to four v. four with two goalkeepers, with each side having a fifth player on the touchline. After each goal, because this practice is quite exhausting, one player of the scoring side goes off with the fifth man replacing him. The players go off in strict rotation.

The playing area should be clearly marked out with full size goals (if possible) at each end. The area should be around 18 yards wide and 25 to 30 yards long.

In a pitch only 25 to 30 yards long the players can shoot very frequently, often first-time, and the coach should emphasise that this is intended to be primarily a shooting practice and that shots should be attempted at even the slightest opportunity.

The four players on each side mark each other in turn as the posesssion of the ball switches, and try to get free when their team gets the ball. This practice is especially good for improving the players ability to receive the ball, turn on it and shoot, all under pressure from an opponent.

ADVICE ON THINGS THAT GO WRONG

1. Shots go too high and over the bar because the upper part of the body is bent too far back when shooting.
2. The supporting leg is too far from the ball resulting in the upper part of the body being over the standing leg and thus preventing the weight of the body being transferred through the ball to add power.
3. The direction of the approach to the ball is incorrect and the kicking foot is therefore wrapped around the ball. This often results in the ball being pulled wide of the target.

   When shooting as the ball approaches from one side or the other, the shoulder is not pointing towards

the goal. If the shoulder is pointing towards the goal this helps to prevent shots going wide.
5. Players fail to get the striking surface of the foot in line with the ball.
6. The knee and ankle joints are not firm enough at the moment of impact with the result that the shot lacks power and may also be off target.

THINGS THAT YOUNG PLAYERS FIND DIFFICULT TO DO
1. Taking their eye off the ball to note the position and movements of the goalkeeper to react accordingly.
2. Swinging the kicking foot in the direction they want the ball to travel.
3. Concentrate on composure and accuracy when they find themselves in a good scoring position.
4. When volleying straight ahead, failing to lean away backwards and point the toe down as far as it will go. Also kicking the ball too early, not waiting until it is as close to the ground as possible. These factors combine to send the ball ballooning over the bar.

HEADING TECHNIQUE
The technique of heading involves the use of the whole body, and the movement begins with the legs. After impact the trunk and the whole of the upper body are thrown forward. The ball is hit with the forehead which is not only the most accurate striking surface but is also the hardest part of the head. Head through the ball and follow through in the direction the ball is intended to travel; chin tucked in, neck muscles taut.

Many young players become frightened of heading because they head the ball with other parts of their head than the forehead. The result can be very painful, and may cause them to go through their career with a fear of heading.

With the ball in the air, jumping should be with a one foot take-off. The last stride before take-off should be a long one with the body leaning back. As the take-off leg extends, the knee of the other leg is swung forward and upwards powerfully. A forward and upwards swing of both arms will assist momentum. Cock the trunk, neck and head ready for heading and both legs should be kicked backwards and upwards. This causes the whole spine to arch backwards and the upper body is jack-knifed forward at the hips and the normal snapping for ward of the head occurs. The ball must be watched carefully right onto the forehead.

The simplest form of practice is to have one ball for two players. The first player throws the ball to his colleague, who heads the ball back.

This practice can be adapted so that the player with the ball throws it up above his head, jumps and heads the ball to his colleague who catches it and repeats.

The easiest introduction to heading a moving ball is to have a ball suspended in the air. The players head the ball, first from a standing position underneath the ball, and then after running at the ball and jumping.

The players can now be introduced to a passing practice, with the players lined up in pairs, one ball between each pair, standing three to five yards apart. The first player serves for himself, throwing the ball up and then heading it to his colleague who heads it back. See how many passes each pair can make in two minutes.

Heading practices

Eight to ten players form themselves into two files with the first man in each file facing each other. One with the ball serves for himself and heads to the player facing him, while each of them run to the back of the opposite files after their headers, the practice continues as each player comes to the front of his file, heading back to the man facing him.

Another simple practice is to have three players and one ball, in a straight line, each player five yards apart. The first player throws the ball up and heads to the middle man who heads it back. The first player then has to head the ball over the middle player to the far man who heads it to the middle man who has turned to face him The practice is repeated without stopping unless the skill breaks down.

To practise heading for distance, three players should be in a straight line about twenty-five yards apart with the outside players having a ball each. The first player chips or lobs the ball for the man in the centre to head back as hard and high as he can. The middle man then turns to face the player at the other end who also chips or lobs a high ball for the middle man to head back. Change the middle man every five minutes.

To develop the ability to head at angles, the same three players can then form themselves into a triangle with one ball. Players A and B form the base-line of the triangle serving the ball for player C who is about twenty-five yards from each player. A chips the ball up for B to head to C. Then player C chips the ball up to B to head to A and repeat. Change the middle man again every five minutes.

Another simple practice is to have the players formed into two files facing each other about ten yards apart. The coach positions himself between the two rows of players about twenty yards away with a supply of balls. At a signal from the coach, the first player in the left file runs towards him and the coach throws the ball up for the player to head the ball back to the coach on the run. The coach then signals to the first player in the right hand file to make his approach and throws for him to head back on the run. After their headers the players form up in two files again, this time behind the coach, ready for working in the opposite direction.

Practice at heading at goal can begin in a very simple form with the coach standing on the penalty spot with a supply of balls and a goalkeeper behind him. A player stands next to a corner flag placed on the penalty area line in front of goal. The coach throws the ball up for the player to run forward and make an attempt to score with a header at goal. After heading the ball the player runs around the flag before the coach throws the next ball for him to have another header. This practice is quite tiring so two minutes will be enough for each player. Count how many goals each player scores in his turn.

Useful practices inevitably become more complicated now. Still heading at goal, four attacking players, A, B, C and D should be disposed at the corners of the penalty area as in Diagram 32. Two players E and F cross the ball from the junction of goal-line and penalty area lines.

E crosses for player C to run forward and head at goal

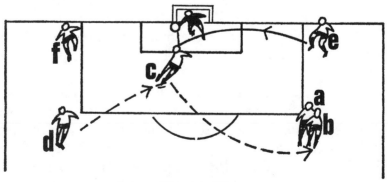

Diagram 32

after which he re-positions with A and B. Then F serves
a ball for A to head at goal and he then joins player D.
E then crosses for D and so on, changing the servers
round every five minutes.

A more match-like practice involves six to ten players
who form themselves into pairs on the halfway-line as in
Diagram 33, one ball to each pair. Player A passes the

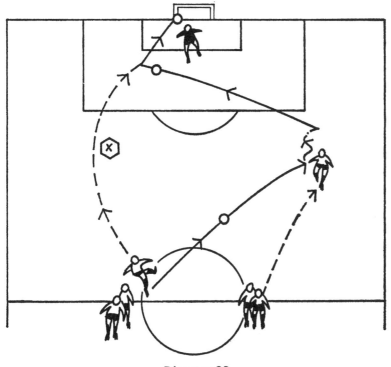

Diagram 33

ball forward for B chasing it to cross the ball. Meanwhile,
after playing the ball, A makes a curved run at goal, first
passing outside a marker X, before making his run at goal
and get in a header. Obviously it is important that the two
players watch each other closely to time the cross correctly. C then plays a similar ball for D, and the practice

continues in pairs with the two players changing roles at intervals.

Curled or bent crosses figure prominently in the game today and to practise them the coach should distribute his players according to Diagram 34. The crossing players

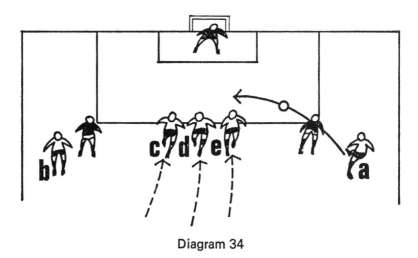

Diagram 34

A and B, have, in turn, to bend their crosses around a defender X. At a signal from the coach, A starts the practice, curling his cross round the defender and varying his crosses by aiming at the far post or near post. Players C, D and E time their runs and attempt to get in scoring headers to beat the goalkeeper who can come out to cut out bad crosses. Once the heading players are re-positioned the coach gives a signal for B to cross, and repeat, changing players A and B over frequently so they all get a turn at curling balls in and everyone gets the heading practice.

Heading for defenders must not be overlooked and a simple practice is to have two serving players taking goal kicks from the corners of the goal area while four defenders spread themselves in defensive positions across the halfway line. In turn, the servers kick out to any area they choose, but alternating them so that all the defenders get practice. The defenders jump to head the ball back to the servers.

There are some special points to watch for:

(a) The decision to head the ball must be made early by one of the defenders.

(b) The timing of the jump is vital so that maximum height is gained as the ball arrives.

(c) The defenders co-operate by talking.

(d) The eyes must be kept open all through the heading action.

(e) The forehead must be thrown at the lower half of the ball for by so doing, "lift" is added to the header to gain height and distance.

A more complicated practice is set out in Diagram 35 with four serving players S and two defenders A and B. The servers each have a ball and hit good long balls into

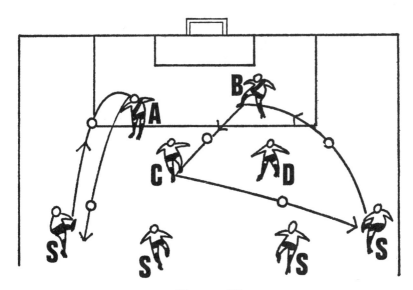

Diagram 35

the penalty area. Players A and B co-operate to clear all
the balls and in so doing each defender has a choice. They
can head the ball directly back to the server, or alternatively, they can head the ball out accurately to either
player C or D in midfield, who, when the ball comes to
them, receive it with close control before returning to the
server.

In Diagram 36, a practice is described for two attackers
against two defenders and a goalkeeper. Players C and D
position like wingers and defenders X await develop-
ments. Meanwhile four to six players form themselves
into pairs as A and B, positioned on the halfway line
and attacking in turn. A and B move forward inter-

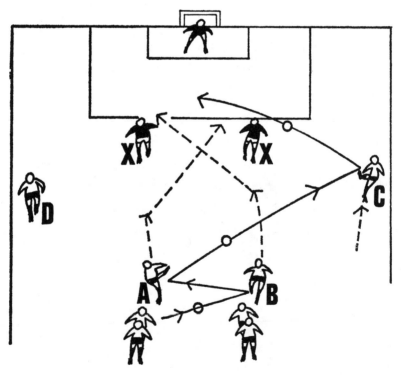

Diagram 36

passing slowly before A gives a long accurate ball to C (B would pass to D). C receives the ball and runs forward with it giving players A and B time to get forward, and then C tries to find A or B with a good cross.

The players are now being compelled to judge the application of heading techniques while being challenged by defenders and at the same time this judgement must take into account the movements of opponents.

When the practice is finished by either a goal being scored or the ball being cleared, the next pair on the halfway line begin inter-passing, this time using player D to cross the ball.

This type of opposed heading practice can be transferred to a small sided game for three v. three and two goalkeepers with full size goals in an area fifty to sixty yards long and thirty to thirty-five yards wide.

The two small sided teams play free football with six more players positioned on the touchlines, one at each corner and one on each side of the halfway line. The six active players can use the players on the outside of the pitch but they are restricted to two touches while the six active players play free football except that goals can only be scored with headers.

When a goal is scored, the successful team regain the ball and resume by attacking the opposite goal. If the ball goes out of play or a foul is committed, encourage quick re-starts. Obviously a three v. three game is both physically and mentally very tiring so after five minutes, the six players positioned on the sidelines should change over and play three v. three, while the original six players position on the touchlines.

Three playing periods of five minutes and three rest periods of five minutes will be enough. Thus, twelve players are involved for thirty minutes.

ADVICE ON THINGS THAT GO WRONG
1. When heading, the chin is not tucked in and the neck muscles are relaxed.
2. The ball is not hit with the forehead.
3. The ball is allowed to hit the head rather than the head hit the ball.
4. The players fail to follow through in the direction they want the ball to travel.
5. The ball is not watched right onto the forehead.
6. Use is not made of the whole body and thus the header lacks power.
7. The ball is hit below its centre point with the top of the forehead.
8. When jumping to head the ball, players take-off from both feet.

THINGS THAT YOUNG PLAYERS CANNOT DO
1. Hit the ball with the correct part of the forehead.
2. Follow through correctly.
3. Make use of the whole body when heading.
4. Judge at what point in the ball's flight, it will be dropping low enough to be headed.

by **Peter Shilton**

Peter Shilton was born at Leicester on 18th September 1949, began training with Leicester City at the age of 11 and remained with them until 1974. Twice transferred for more than £300,000 to Stoke City and then to Nottingham Forest, he first played for England in 1970.

He played a vital part in helping Nottingham Forest win the First Division championship in season 1977–78, and many knowledgeable critics are of the opinion that he is the best goalkeeper in Britain.

Continental European goalkeepers have clearly improved in recent years but for a long time, they and their coaches seemed more concerned with developing the ability to make spectacular saves.

In Britain where the high cross has always been an integral part of the game, the goalkeeper has had to play a much greater part in the defence as a unit, and has therefore developed all round qualities that continental goalkeepers did not have.

Goalkeeping is an art quite apart from the outfield positions in soccer and no matter what the range of other qualities a player may have, he will never make a top class goalkeeper without courage. Two situations which highlight this crop up repeatedly.

Dealing with high crosses is something a good goalkeeper must be good at, but I have occasionally seen a goalkeeper go out to a high ball with one eye on the ball, and the other on a striker coming to challenge in the air. In this situation the goalkeeper can often miss the ball completely with disastrous results.

Secondly, there are times when the goalkeeper has to go out to dive at the feet of an opponent who has broken through the defence. The forward can pull out of the challenge if he feels there is the risk of injury, but that is a luxury that the goalkeeper cannot afford.

So cold courage is a prime quality in goalkeeping, and there is simply no substitute for it.

DEALING WITH HIGH CROSSES

The goalkeeper has one big advantage over all other players when facing a high cross or a corner. He can use his hands. So one of the basics of good goalkeeping is to make full use of this advantage for these situations can be very dangerous for defences, and here the goalkeeper must dominate.

The goalkeeper must go as far as possible to meet the ball and take it at its highest point with the arms fully stretched. Jumping high with the arms fully extended to meet the ball, the goalkeeper can reach the ball at a much higher point than the height at which any forward can head it.

So the goalkeeper must make the maximum use of this advantage and aim to catch the ball at a good height above the heads.

A common fault with inexperienced goalkeepers is that they allow the ball to drop to head height before trying to intercept it. Catching the ball with the arms bent at head height is a common fault amongst young goalkeepers and a simple practice will help.

Two goalkeepers can work together, throwing high balls to each other from around fifteen yards. The coach should insist that they go to meet the ball and catch it with arms fully extended and once they have mastered this habit the goalkeepers can gradually work back to twenty yards and twenty-five yards. The fault is usually one of timing the approach to the ball, and practice will improve this.

So to deal with the high cross the goalkeeper must watch the ball only and go for it with courage and confidence, aiming to reach the ball at the highest possible point. Once he has committed himself to going for the ball, the goalkeeper must go all the way whatever happens. If he has misjudged his approach slightly, or is impeded, he can fall back on the punch, but to stop halfway out will probably be fatal. Once committed he must go all the way.

The coach should see to it that the goalkeeper gets regular practice at dealing with high crosses, bringing in other players to help. Crosses should be put in from both the right wing and the left wing, and from all angles. They should also be varied so that the goalkeeper has practice at dealing with crosses aimed at the far post and the near post.

Once the goalkeeper has developed the technique of meeting the ball at its highest point an opponent can be introduced to try and score. This opposition could be provided by the reserve goalkeeper and after ten to fifteen minutes practice the two goalkeepers can change places.

Dealing with corner kicks and free kicks from a narrow angle near the corner flag is no different to a cross in fluid play except that the goalkeeper has more time to position himself.

In my opinion the goalkeeper should have a full back covering each post to leave him free to go out for the high cross. He should position himself about two yards off the goal-line and two yards out from the far post. From there, he can take a step back and jump to deal with the ball aimed at the far post, and being two yards out already he is on his way to deal with a cross anywhere in the goal-mouth.

It is impossible to lay down hard and fast rules for all crosses, corners and free kicks from narrow angles, but one point should always be borne in mind: it is easier to go forward to meet the ball than it is to go backwards and everyone can always jump higher when going forward than they can when shuffling backwards. This point should help the goalkeeper determine exactly where he should position himself.

One of the most difficult crosses to deal with is the one driven hard and low into the goalmouth from a point close to the goal-line, and it will be all the more difficult to deal with on a wet and greasy surface for the ball will tend to skid off the wet turf at an unpredictable speed.

With an opponent in possession close to the goal-line, the goalkeeper should position himself at the near post and try to smother the ball by diving on it, if it comes in low.

Most goalkeepers will find that they can naturally get down faster to the left or to the right, and a good practice to improve on this is to have two players working with the goalkeeper. The first player should be around ten yards from the near post on the goal-line and drive the ball in hard and low. On the other side of the penalty area should be another player. If the goalkeeper is beaten this other player will retrieve the ball, dribble it in until he is about ten yards from the other post and then drive the ball back in from that side. While he is controlling the ball and getting into a crossing position the goalkeeper should have time to get across his goal and cover the other post and again he tries to dive on the ball.

If the goalkeeper saves the ball, he throws it out to the

opposite side and then moves to cover the near post each time.

There will however be times when the goalkeeper cannot get to the near post and have the chance to smother the ball there; for example when the ball is crossed from one wing and the ball flies over the goalmouth to drop on the far side of the goal and is immediately driven back in hard and low.

So the goalkeeper has two possibilities. He can go forward to the near post area and go down to smother the ball, or he can wait and try to make a reflex save.

If the goalkeeper has no time to get to the near post he can still go down in the goalmouth which requires a lot of courage for this is one of the most difficult situations in the game. Alternatively he can wait and try to save any shot that comes, and if he is not sure that he can dive on the ball he will probably be best advised to wait.

PUNCHING THE BALL

When dealing with high balls, punching is clearly second best to catching. Catch the ball and all danger is over whereas the punch gives only temporary relief. Yet despite the obvious advantage of catching there is still a place for punching.

There will be times when other players obstruct the goalkeeper, for example when a defender is going up with an opponent trying to head the ball, or when the goalkeeper's view may have been obstructed by an opponent until the last moment. In these situations the punch can be invaluable.

If the circumstances make it difficult or impossible for the goalkeeper to catch the ball cleanly, then he must punch the ball as high and as far as he can, preferably away towards the wings.

There are however a number of different punches and each one should be practised.

To deal with a ball lobbed up the middle or angled in from the flanks, the goalkeeper should use a two fisted punch to get the ball as far away as possible.

For this two fisted practice the coach can get two goalkeepers to work together, alternately serving and punching for five minutes each. The ball can be served by lobbing it up with a drop kick out of the hands, straight up the middle and also from slightly to the left and the right.

The goalkeeper having practice should go to meet the ball as high as possible and using a two fisted punch, propel the ball back to the server who should be about thirty yards away.

With a high cross, if the goalkeeper cannot catch the ball or even deliver a two fisted punch, the best solution will be to help the ball on its way. Meeting the ball as high as possible, the power of a one fisted punch should be added to the velocity of the ball by deflecting its path, as in Diagram 37, sending the ball as far as possible out towards the opposite wing from which the ball came.

Punching the ball over the bar is a different technique altogether and should only be employed in real emergencies. Two goalkeepers can work together to practise

Diagram 37

this skill, with one serving by throwing the ball from around fifteen yards so that the ball is dropping in the region of the crossbar or would even hit it.

Imagining that the goalkeeper is under pressure from one or more opponents and cannot safely catch the ball, fisting it over the bar is the only practical solution.

The server should start at one side of the goal line and serve the ball into the region of the bar, working slowly round the goal until he reaches the other side of the goal line. Each time the goalkeeper fists the ball over the bar. Then the two goalkeepers can change places.

Having developed the different punching techniques, the best practice will be for the coach to supervise the goalkeeper in a crowded goalmouth. Crosses should be put in from alternate wings and from different angles.

With a lot of bodies in the goal area the goalkeeper will probably find it difficult to make a safe catch, but he should do so whenever possible. When this is impractical for any reason then he must select the appropriate punch and deal with every situation on its merits.

The coach should offer praise for a good catch or punch, but also point out the error when a bad selection is made or for a poor skill performance. If the coach notes that the goalkeeper is particularly weak at dealing with one type of cross he can ask the players serving the ball to concentrate on the troublesome ball, and if the goalkeeper shows a weakness in one of the different punching techniques he should get the two goalkeepers to practise it together later.

This practice with his fellow defenders opposed by four or five strikers is very important, for the goalkeeper must learn to dominate the penalty area and also call good advice to his colleagues.

Whenever the goalkeeper goes out for the ball he

should call "keeper's ball" to let everyone know he is coming.

Because the goalkeeper is the last line in defence, he can survey almost the entire defensive area. Apart from calling loudly that he is coming whenever he leaves his line, the good goalkeeper can give advice to all his colleagues.

If the goalkeeper is not going for the ball and a colleague is about to be challenged, particularly by someone from his blind side, the goalkeeper can call "clear it". He can also call "hold it" to a defender who has no one near him.

The good goalkeeper must dominate the other defensive players and be in command of the penalty area, which he must regard as his domain. He must call good advice in plenty of time to all his colleagues according to the situation and must go for everything he thinks he can reach.

Giving good advice, the goalkeeper will earn the respect of his defensive colleagues, and they will look upon him as the boss of the penalty area. But to gain this respect, the goalkeeper must deal with everything he goes for in the air, and often risk injury by going down in the goalmouth at an opponent's feet. When the goalkeeper goes for the ball he cannot afford to fail to deal with the situation.

Too many goalkeepers are what I call line-keepers. They merely stay on their line, going for crosses if they are close enough, but generally only waiting for shots to be fired at them, when they will attempt to make a spectacular save.

DISTRIBUTION

The last man in defence, the goalkeeper is also the first man in attack. It is no good making a fantastic save and then kicking the ball out to an opponent who uses it to start an attack that leads to a goal.

A good goalkeeper must distribute the ball well, and he can often start a move that leads to a goal at the other end.

Of the various ways for a goalkeeper to distribute the ball, the most commonly used is the volley out of the hands. If he can volley kick the ball accurately and drop it onto the head of a colleague, or at his feet, then this is clearly an advantage. If he can kick the ball a bit further now and again so that the ball drops beyond the line of opposing defenders so much the better. With the four paces law, and some forwards keen on standing on the goalkeeper's strongest kicking side, it is also necessary to be able to kick the ball at least reasonably well with the weaker foot too.

Two goalkeepers can practise this volley kicking together, volleying to each other and not forgetting to practise with their weaker foot.

With the goal-kick there are two alternatives. The first is to give the ball a long punt upfield aimed for a colleague, and the second alternative is to play a short kick out to a defender who returns the ball so that the goalkeeper can volley the ball upfield.

Personally I prefer the second method because I can get more distance and also more accuracy with my volley kicking. But again, two goalkeepers should practise taking dead ball kicks to each other.

Accuracy can always be improved with practice, and the coach should supervise two goalkeepers kicking to each other over various distances. The most important thing to look for is that the kicker must keep his eye on the ball. Immediately before the kick, the goalkeeper lifts his gaze to take in a mental picture of the field and the players. Then eyes back on the ball and keep them there, throughout the kick until after the follow through.

THROWING THE BALL OUT

As an alternative to kicking, the goalkeeper can also throw the ball out to colleagues in three main ways.

1. A short quick throw, usually an under-arm roll, to a defender who is well positioned to start an attack.
2. The low throw to a team-mate in midfield. This throw should be kept low and thrown hard, so that the opposition does not have time to intercept.

Always call to the player that the throw is intended for with these two throws for I have seen throws directed to players who are not expecting the ball to be thrown to them and are turning away at the time. The consequences can be disastrous if this happens, but there should be no danger if the goalkeeper calls to the player by name as he throws the ball.

A longer type throw is used by some goalkeepers instead of the volley kick out of the hands and some of the best can throw the ball almost as far as they can kick it.

Unless the goalkeeper has the right physique—long arms and powerful muscles—it should be discouraged, but throwing for length and accuracy can again be improved if two goalkeepers practise this together. Though I prefer to volley the ball, players with an exceptionally good throw should be encouraged to use it.

The essential thing is that having halted an attack by winning the ball, the goalkeeper can often find a colleague near the halfway line who has been left relatively unmarked as the opponents pushed up to attack. If the goalkeeper can get the ball to him quickly and accurately it will be a big advantage. Observation of the goalkeeper in matches will reveal whether he can throw the ball accurately over long distances and if he can the coach should allow him to continue—and practise.

FREE KICKS

Facing a free kick close to goal it is the goalkeeper's responsibility to supervise the defensive wall. As in Diagram 38 the human wall should be constructed in such a way that it covers the direct shot to the nearest post, while the goalkeeper is responsible for the direct shot at the rest of the goal, and he must make sure that he is not unsighted.

More and more players are now trying to "bend" the ball around the wall so I prefer to have five men in the wall, with an extra man on the end to block the "bent" shot. The goalkeeper must go to the near post and make sure the wall is in the right place before positioning himself.

How much space the goalkeeper leaves for himself to cover depends on the angle of the kick and on his own ability. He should assume responsibility for covering more of the goal if the kick is to be taken from well out, and look to the wall to cover more of the goal if the kick is to be from closer in.

Diagram 38

In addition to the "bent" shot, the goalkeeper should be alert and watch for the ball chipped over the wall that will drop in flight into the goal in the region of the angle of post and bar in the near post area.

An alert and agile goalkeeper should however be able to get across behind the wall and save a chip shot, for by its very nature it travels more slowly than a direct shot that can be hammered in.

With a free kick from a narrow angle I like to have a two man wall to cover the direct shot at the near post area. Then I position myself a few yards off the goal line so that I can cover as much of the penalty area as possible in case the ball is crossed for a header or shot.

I keep to the same basic approach whether the free kick is direct or indirect, but for the indirect kick the defenders in the wall must be ready to break and offer a quick challenge to anyone the ball is passed to, while the goalkeeper must be ready to spring forward to deal with the ball if it is chipped into the goalmouth.

To avoid any confusion, because time is limited, the coach should nominate before the game which players should be the five to make up the wall.

NARROWING THE ANGLE

With a player in a shooting position just inside the penalty area the goalkeeper has little chance to save a good, hard shot aimed just inside either post if he stays on the goal line. But if he goes out to narrow the angle then the goalkeeper has only half the distance (or less) to dive to save the same shot as is clearly shown in Diagram 39.

That is the principle, but obviously it is not as easy as that. If the goalkeeper advances too far there is the danger of seeing the ball lobbed over his head.

If an opponent looks like shooting from around thirty

Diagram 39

yards it is enough to position only around two to three yards off the line. From there the goalkeeper should be able to save an attempted lob shot or chip, and with the longer type shot there is more time to get across goal and save.

It follows then that with a shot from closer in, say the edge of the penalty area, there is less time to move and save, so the goalkeeper will have to narrow the angle much more.

So the goalkeeper must use his intelligence and sense of anticipation in every situation and position himself so that he can always fall back to cover the chip shot, and yet be finely balanced to dive to either side to save.

There is one other point to take into consideration when anticipating a shot. This is not to get too close to the opponent. An extreme case will serve to underline this: if the goalkeeper is seven yards out to an opponent with the ball who is only ten yards out, the goalkeeper is too close to have time to see the shot and save.

A very good practice to help goalkeepers learn to position themselves correctly when narrowing the angle is to have players positioned all round the goal at a distance of eighteen yards as in Diagram 40.

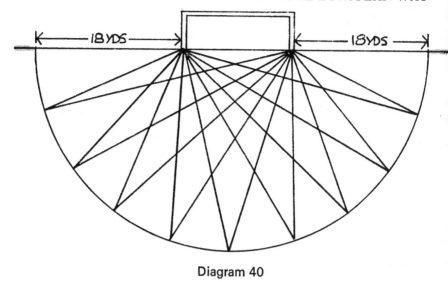

Diagram 40

At the instruction of the coach, each player shoots in turn, and the goalkeeper has to narrow the angle and position himself correctly for every shot. If the goalkeeper comes out too far, the shooting player can try to chip the ball over his head into goal while the coach can offer comments on his positioning.

If observation of this practice reveals that the goalkeeper is being beaten more often from one particular angle, the coach can look to see what he is doing wrong and devote extra time to fielding shots from that particular angle. Generally a right-handed goalkeeper will be better at going down to save with his right hand (and vice versa), and if there is a weakness on one side or the other, extra practice will help.

GOING DOWN AT FEET

Perhaps the most challenging aspect of goalkeeping is the moment when an opponent has broken through on his own, or been put away with a through pass and the goalkeeper has to go out to meet him and go down at his feet. A good striker should usually win such a one v. one duel, but with intelligence and anticipation a good goalkeeper can do much to cut down on his chances. The worst thing a goalkeeper can do is to rush out blindly. Advance to meet him carefully, in a semi-crouching position. In that way, whether he tries to dribble past the goalkeeper or push the ball past him, he is nicely balanced and well positioned to block the ball.

All goalkeepers know that there will be times when this situation arises and he will get more than his share of bumps and bruises. So courage is a vital ingredient in the good goalkeeper and he must take these situations as part of the game.

If the goalkeeper can get close enough to the striker, go down for the ball with the arms stretched out towards it and the body behind the ball. Tuck the head well down to minimise the chances of serious injury. But there is no substitute for cold courage.

The coach can give the goalkeeper practice at this by asking the strikers to run at the goal with the ball at their feet, starting from the edge of the penalty area and the goalkeeper on his line. The strikers must not shoot but must try to go round the goalkeeper and walk the ball into the net while the goalkeeper tries to dispossess them by diving at their feet.

The practice should then be switched so that a striker starts off with the ball from one wing, dribbling towards goal and trying to score, and the next striker positioned slightly more towards the centre.

If the strikers set off from different positions, working right through the complete 180 degrees, the goalkeeper will get practice at dealing with an opponent who approaches goal from his right, from his left and through the middle.

Again, if the goalkeeper concedes more goals from one or two angles, the coach should give him extra practice at dealing with the situations that prove to be most difficult for him.

CONCENTRATION AND ANTICIPATION

Even if the goalkeeper has little or nothing to do for lengthy periods he has to develop the ability to concentrate on the game, just like the other ten outfield players.

If the goalkeeper can read the game like his defensive colleagues he should be able to anticipate just where and when the high cross is coming, and be halfway out to meet it.

Similarly, the goalkeeper can try to anticipate the through ball that splits his defence, and be halfway out when the pass is made. If the goalkeeper waits for things to happen he will probably be too late to do very much about the difficult situations that arise in and around the penalty area.

When the play is at the far end of the pitch, the goalkeeper can safely position himself well off his line. Then if a long pass is made and an enemy forward breaks away, he is well positioned, even to go outside the penalty area and kick the ball away.

Through concentration and anticipation, the goalkeeper can sense when a pass is going to beat the line of defenders, or when an opponent is going to win a ball in the air and head it on towards goal. One can repeatedly see good goalkeepers who have anticipated these situations, out on the edge of the eighteen yard area, catching balls with an opponent just a few feet away. If the goalkeeper had not been out there, he would possibly have had to face a one v. one situation inside the penalty area.

The foresight to anticipate what is going to happen is a sixth sense that all the good goalkeepers have, anticipating what might happen and positioning themselves accordingly.

AGILITY

Everyone in the team needs to be basically fit to play soccer, but goalkeepers need extra agility over and above the qualities of the other players. For this reason I have always done extra training in a gymnasium.

Clearly however, not all goalkeepers have the use of a gym and for them the next best thing will be the right kind of practice.

The advantage of extra agility is that the goalkeeper will be able to dive and save, and then be able to recover quickly, ready to dive and save again. The best idea is to have two goalkeepers working together, one in goal and the other providing the service. If the goalkeeper is forced to dive first to his left, recover quickly and then dive to his right, this will help to improve his agility.

So the serving goalkeeper should throw the ball from around ten yards, delivering it wide of the goalkeeper, say four yards to his left. The goalkeeper must dive to save the ball and then release it at once so that the server can immediately throw the ball four yards to his right.

After twenty throws (ten to each side) the two goalkeepers can change places. The first throws should be received at something like waist height, and after both goalkeepers have had a stint at serving and saving, they can then serve twenty higher balls to each other, and then twenty low balls, and repeat. Diving first one way, and having to recover quickly and then diving the other way will greatly improve the fitness, agility and energy of the goalkeeper.

PRE-SEASON AND FITNESS TRAINING

When the other players are training for basic fitness especially in pre-season training, but also during the season, it will help the goalkeeper if he joins in. But when the outfield players have a break from fitness training, to practise skills like heading then the goalkeepers should leave the main group and practise on their own.

The aim should be to practise everything that a goalkeeper is called upon to do in matches, and working together, one providing the service, goalkeepers can improve their basic skills.

PRACTICE WITH OTHER DEFENDERS

Although goalkeeping is unique in soccer and demands different qualities from outfield players, the goalkeeper is a vital part of the defence. It follows therefore that it will help to develop understanding if the complete defence can practise as a unit, for example in a game of defence against attack.

Now the goalkeeper can use all his skills at collecting high crosses, going down at feet, calling to his colleagues and making saves etc., all under the supervision of the coach in match like conditions.

Here the coach has an opportunity to re-create situations if he feels the defence needs extra practice at dealing with one aspect of the game. For example he can whistle frequently for imaginary fouls, thus giving a free kick anywhere he chooses to the attacking players that will enable the defence to organise itself quickly in things like building a wall to face the free kick.

The coach can also award corners at will if he thinks the defence, and the goalkeeper in particular need practice at dealing with them. The more the defence plays together as a unit, the better will be their understanding in the collective sense for this is the closest one can get to match like conditions during a training session.

9/ Training for Speed and Stamina

by **Cyril Lea**

Cyril Lea was born at Wrexham on 5th August 1934 and earned an amateur cap for Wales. As a professional he played for Leyton Orient from 1957 before moving in 1964 to Ipswich Town where he gained a Division Two championship medal.

While still playing he began coaching the reserve team and after a three-year course in Physical Training is now a qualified gymnast and physiotherapist.

For a short period he was senior coach in charge of Ipswich Town who were without a manager until Bobby Robson arrived and after that was his assistant with Ipswich Town winning the FA Cup in 1978 after coming close to honours in several earlier seasons. In 1979 he became the coach of Stoke City.

Cyril Lea is also the coach of Wales, forming a successful manager-coach relationship with Mike Smith. He began as part-time coach of Wales under Dave Bowen in 1971 and despite having relatively few First-Division first team players qualified for Wales, achieved the distinction of helping Wales become the only British team to reach the quarter finals of the 1976 European Championship.

If English players have sometimes been less than successful against continental European opposition, their fitness and fighting spirit, as well as the ability to compete for ninety minutes, and more, have never been in doubt.

Indeed the fitness and stamina of the average English

professional has long been the envy of the entire football world.

Coaches come from all over the world to study these aspects of training in the English game and if therefore, continental coaches are better qualified to write about other aspects of the game, the English are so superior in their preparation of players for speed and stamina that this contribution had to be from a man with wide experience in the English game.

Cyril Lea was chosen because he works at both club level and in the international arena with Wales.

TRAINING FOR SPEED

I have always been a great believer in the use of running spikes because it is important to improve the sprinting action in order to improve the speed of players. The technique of sprinting is very important but we do not want to confuse sprinting with athletics because that is quite different to the requirements of soccer. I use spikes because I have found that it helps to give the players a better arm and leg action.

With spikes, players are more conscious of the sprinting action and the use of spikes throws the players forward onto their toes. Through training with spikes I have found that players who lacked initial explosive power have improved.

Real sprinters are born, but for the purposes of soccer the players can certainly improve their sprinting technique and explosive power. Getting off the mark quickly is important for soccer, as is getting from A to B in a shorter time, and this means getting the body weight into its top speed more quickly. We train for speed once or twice every week with all of our players and when a 16-year-old first comes to us we issue him with a set of spikes. Good spikes can be very expensive but amateur players who will not use them so much could make do with a cheaper pair for they will not wear out so quickly.

Training with weights can also improve explosive power but unless the club has someone qualified with weights it will be best to avoid the risk of back injuries and instead of weight training, improve the explosive power with the exercises given below.

In the early stages when the players first put on their spikes we look for a good arm and leg action. Then we need to improve the rhythm of the sprinting, trying to increase the length of the stride BUT KEEP THE SAME RUNNING RHYTHM. It is also very important that the player keeps his muscles relaxed. We vary the training between explosive sprinting over ten yards; rhythm sprinting over 50 to 100 yards and competitive races.

To improve the explosive power, get the players to sprint ten yards from different positions like laying on the ground, then at a signal getting up and exploding. This can be repeated from a sitting position; down on one knee; crouching down; on both knees and turning—all to sprint ten yards with spikes.

Soccer is an explosive game and though a player is born with his speed he can get himself to top speed in a shorter space of time with explosive power. Through training he can get his body weight into top speed quicker because he has got more thrust.

Once the player has got into top speed it is a question of keeping his improved rhythm and running at top speed—relaxed if he can. If the player tries to go faster it will be found that the muscles tighten up and he slows down. So it is a question of holding the rhythm through the run.

With spikes we go on to do 220 yards and 440 yards but that is a build up to stamina work. For speed we concentrate on shorter distances from ten to one hundred yards.

The muscles on top of the thighs are important for explosive power and a good exercise to build up these muscles is to get the players in a position where they "sit" on an imaginary chair with their backs flush against a wall. With feet together and the rear as low as if they really were sitting on a chair, that puts the body weight through the pelvis and onto the thigh muscles. Done properly it is quite a strong exercise and we hold that position for one minute. As you build up, the players can go into three one minute sessions with a short rest between each minute.

One leg squats are also very good. The player extends one leg in front of the body and goes down into a very low squat with the body weight on the other leg. The position to aim for is again as chair-like as possible with the rear almost touching the ground. Up and down, ten squats is the number to aim for. Ten on each leg.

One leg hopping and one leg jumping are other explosive exercises that can be done without weights. Jumping over a stick on one leg; hopping over a stick. Rebound jumping is also very good. Jumping off a stool or bench, or even a table and then jumping over something else before taking a step. So the player jumps down and as he lands he jumps again, throwing the body weight down on the first jump and then getting the body weight to jump again.

A form of interval training can be introduced into the sprinting practice by splitting the players into equal groups about 100 yards apart around the pitch. The first group sprints 100 yards to the second group who then do 100 yards to the third group and carry this on for about ten minutes, with the first group resting until it is their turn again to sprint.

In all sprinting sessions, think first of running technique then of rhythm. Get the players to build up a good rhythm over fifty to one hundred yards, with a good arm and leg action and a good strong stride.

Sometimes you can see that the players feel a bit tight so concentrate on the rhythm. And with the explosive runs emphasise the importance of a good running action, not sprinting and trying to beat someone else.

TRAINING FOR STAMINA

The basis of the season's work is laid down in the pre-season period. Once the league programme has started it should be only a question of keeping the players at peak fitness for I aim to achieve the best possible physical condition when we start our league games.

During the season our weekly training programme will vary according to whether or not we have a game in mid-week and our performances will be another decisive factor.

During the season we will work in much the same way as in pre-season but not of course to the same degree on intensity. But our training activities will be drawn from those used in pre-season training.

For part-time players and boys of the age group 15 to 18 there is no short cut to obtaining a good level of fitness and I feel at least two sessions a week must be aimed for. Assuming the players are enthusiastic, the coach should draw up a varied programme in order that the players should not be discouraged from enjoying the game.

Fitness training may be with and without the ball; relay running of 50 yards, 100 yards and 220 yards; maze running, agility circuits and small sided games will all help to achieve a certain level of fitness.

It cannot be emphasised too much however that the

coach should make the training sessions enjoyable, stimulating, competitive and interesting. Always remember that the use of a ball in stamina training can help to make the hard work enjoyable.

The return to training after a lay off, as in pre-season has to be a well balanced programme so as not to create any unnecessary injuries for example blisters, groin and hamstring strains.

We use the swimming pool quite early to relax aching muscles and everyone has to use the pool for this purpose. Footbaths with skin hardener are used as a precaution against blisters. It should also be noted that the use of talcum powder in the boots helps to absorb sweat and helps to prevent blisters. One important point rarely mentioned is that socks which have a darn in the foot should never be used because this brings an added danger of rubbing in a blister.

Before going into detail with our pre-season programme it should be noted that coaches of amateur teams must scale down the work load compared with professionals. For example where we may run three miles, scale it down to one mile, and if we work at a given activity for fifteen minutes, scale it down to five minutes.

We usually begin our pre-season training on a Wednesday so that after the first three days of work, the players have a free week-end in which to recover.

We always begin our training sessions with a twenty-minute warming up. The players start by jogging, jumping, twisting sideways, turning, touching the ground as they run.

Then we do groin and stretching exercises for the hamstrings are particularly vulnerable after the off-season rest.

For groin exercises open the legs very wide and put the hands on the base of the back. Pushing the pelvis forward then helps to stretch the groins out. The wider the legs are opened, the stronger the exercise. Then, still pushing your hips forward, lift the legs alternately, putting each leg out wide and moving it in a big circular movement, stretching the groins out again.

First day—Wednesday
Morning:
We start by running from the ground to a local park which is about two miles away. Once there we do short running activities in groups so that the players get a little break when their group is resting.

Then we introduce the ball for thirty minutes with the players in groups. They do things like:

(a) Throwing the ball to each other.

(b) Giving first time passes, pass and move, pass and move.

(c) Working in a circle playing one touch football.

The groups change activities at ten minute intervals so they all do each activity.

After that we do abdominal exercises.

Lying on their backs the players have their hands behind their head. Head and shoulders raising to a sitting position about thirty times.

After a few moments relaxation the players lay on their backs again with the hands on the thighs. Head and shoulders raising to touch the knees with the hands, again about thirty times.

Finally, legs raising and with hands stretched out above the head, hands raising to touch the toes in a jack-knife position. Again about thirty times.

It is hard work but the players get used to it.

Then we do one run of 440 yards, not a sprint just a good strong run. Then run in to the ground, another 2 miles.

Afternoon:

Warm up for about twenty minutes with groin exercises and stretching as already described. Then jogging interspersed with jumping, turning, twisting, running sideways and backwards.

For 45 minutes, the players break up into groups and do various skill practices with the ball, moving round the groups so that all players do everything. Nothing complicated just basic skills.

Then the players break up into groups of six and for twenty minutes play games six v. six.

After that they finish with one hard run for twelve minutes.

Second day—Thursday

Morning:

We start with a four mile run and then just to break away from running we include the ball to break up the running activity. This gives the players a little chance to recover but still keep them occupied. Ball work will be the same as the previous day but it gets the players minds off their legs and onto the ball for about thirty minutes.

Back to running again and this time we try to keep up a good pace by splitting the players into groups. All the players run together but in their distinct groups and at the start the coach nominates one group to lead. As soon as the leading group starts to flag—after about three minutes —the coach nominates another group to sprint to the front and take over to set the pace. The park we train in is about two miles wide so we might run straight for about one mile but the leading group can run anywhere they wish.

Changing the leading group every three minutes keeps up the quality of the running which is not intended to be a sprint, just a good pace. To complete the morning's work we do some running uphill and downhill. We start with six uphill runs and work up to ten and make it competitive. In small groups about five yards apart and running in competition against the other group. Hill climbs help to build up stamina and the players jog back down. Running downhill they let the limbs go to loosen off because running downhill is really relaxing.

The morning's work will total about one and a half hours.

Afternoon:

After warming up we will have a session on agility work and ball skills. For the agility work each player has a ball and standing beside it he will do various forms of body movements. Jumping over the ball, astride jumping, then jumping backwards and forwards over the ball.

Then, working in pairs with one player serving, the other player will have to get up first from a sitting position to jump and head the ball back, and then do the same thing from a squatting position. Of course the players change over so that each one serves and jumps.

The skill practices will be working at all the basic things the players do in the game: passing, trapping, dribbling, shooting, heading, shielding, and generally getting the feel of the ball.

All this will take about forty-five minutes and then we will have the players split into groups again for six v. six games for twenty minutes.

Again we will finish off with one hard run for twelve minutes.

Third day—Friday

Morning:

The players will start with a five mile cross-country run and finish off with more running uphill and downhill.

The afternoon will be free and with Saturday and Sunday will give the players a chance to recover.

Fourth day—Monday

Morning:

In pairs the players will do a running circuit on an interval training basis. Alternately they will sprint ten yards; twenty yards; fifty yards and one hundred yards. One working, one resting. The total distance will be about 1,500 yards.

After the running we introduce the ball again for skill practices.

In two lines the players head the ball back and forth, keeping it up as long as possible. We try to make all skills competitive so each group works against the others. For example the last group to keep the ball up wins. Then they do the same thing in pairs, again competitive.

Then they have a ball each and using any part of the body allowed in the game, keep the ball up as long as possible.

Still on skills the players pair off but forming a circle with one of each pair with a ball around the group of heading players. The heading players inside the circle have to pick out their ball as it is thrown and work first for long defensive heading and then for powerful heading down as at goal. After five minutes the players change roles, varying the service so that the heading player has to get up for high balls and head a low ball powerfully back to the server.

After this we pair off the players for shooting practice under pressure. One player has a one yard start and has to reach a served ball and shoot before he is caught by his partner. The players alternate shooting and chasing.

Having recovered from the first physical session of the morning we will then do a Fartlek circuit for about two miles. The players begin with running at a steady pace for fifty yards, then sprint for fifty yards alternately, just breaking up the rhythm of the running and trying to increase the pace in the sprint sections. Two miles is about six laps of the pitch.

Then all the players go to the swimming pool for twenty minutes to relax.

Afternoon:

The players warm up individually as they prefer. Then they are divided into three groups, each group working at one of the activities below and changing over after about thirty minutes:

Group one: sprinting over hurdles spaced at intervals over two hundred yards on a competitive basis. Six hurdles to be cleared on the run out, going in pairs, and sprinting straight back. Players rest while the others go, then sprint again.

Group two: agility work with partners with one ball between two. Begin by taking the ball between the player's two feet and by jumping up and bending the knees, flick the ball up to the rear. Repeat ten times each.

Then still working in pairs, the server throws the ball up in any direction and the "working" player has to reach the pitch of the ball and return it by kicking it back to the server after one bounce. At the command of the coach this can be changed to having the player return the ball before it touches the ground, but obviously the serve will have to be suitable. Begin with thirty seconds each and build up to one minute each and spend most time on returning the ball after one bounce.

This practice improves the reflexes and agility of the players who have to turn and sprint to reach the ball, then often have to hit the ball on the turn to prevent it bouncing a second time.

Group three: playing in five v. two games with varied

conditions. Start with two touch, then outside of the foot only, then inside of the foot only. Total time about one and a half hours.

Fifth day—Tuesday
Morning:
Warm up individually as preferred.

Players divided into three groups, each group working for twenty minutes at the three activities given below. Total time one hour.

(a) Six v. six game . . . keep ball.
(b) Shooting practice—in pairs, serving and shooting alternately after ten shots. Shooting on the volley, half volley and on the turn.
(c) Ball skills. In pairs with serving players on the outside of a circle. The serving player has to find his partner among the group of players with a pass according to the instructions of the coach. Two touch, first time, inside or outside of the foot, heading or continuous passing.

For another thirty minutes work according to the condition of the players. If they are physically tired after the previous day's work, organise six v. six games with goals which will be enjoyable but still keep the players active. If they do not seem to be shattered, introduce some form of running activity.

Afternoon:
For the first twenty minutes, abdominal work as already described.

Then the players each do timed runs:
440 yards—twice. Expected time 70 seconds.
220 yards—three times each. Expected time 32 seconds.
100 yards—six times each. Expected time 15 seconds.

Players rest while others run. Each player exhorted to do better than his previous time.

Sixth day—Wednesday

Morning:

Eleven a side practice match. Three thirty minute periods. During breaks make points that have been observed. Coach might even stop the game from time to time to emphasise points that crop up.

Swimming. Twenty minutes.

Afternoon:

Agility circuit for thirty minutes. Working with a partner, one minute work and one minute rest. Working at twelve stations and perform different exercises at each one using wall bars, mats, benches; jumping, squats, stomach exercises etc., sprinting from one exercise to the next.

If a gymnasium is not available, players can be asked to jump any suitable object like a row of chairs; do a long jump over a marked distance, and do exercises like squats, jumping as if to head a ball, abdominal exercises etc. Small sided games, five v. five for thirty minutes.

Seventh day—Thursday

Morning:

Eight v. eight games with conditions. For example, first time passing, two touch, or possession football. Then for thirty minutes, running activities with the ball.

1. Players working in threes with two players at ends fifty yards apart. The third player starts between them with a ball, running at a good pace with good ball control. When he reaches the end of the fifty-yard section, the waiting player collects the ball and runs to the far man at a good pace with good control and when he gets to the far end the third man runs. Repeat and keep going.

2. Two groups of players in Indian file fifteen yards

apart. First time passing to the front man in opposite file. After passing the player sprints to the end of the opposite file. Keep going.

Less skilled players could do this with two touches.

The object here is really to get the feel of the ball and the quality of the passing has to be emphasised. This is used as a less strenuous activity after a match when the players are tired and think they have had enough. Really to show the players that you can get a bit more out of them than they thought they could give you.

Twenty minutes swimming.

Afternoon:

After warming up, running and sprint session.

First, running with twists and turns; backward running; sideways running; running with high jumps included and at a signal, turning to touch the player behind then sprinting away for ten yards.

Running in pairs and at a signal the players turn and sprint, trying to get past the pair now in front of them. Alternate this with having each pair in front having to try and touch the pair behind them who sprint away at a signal from the coach.

Break off the running and do stomach exercises. Lying on their backs hands above the head and coming up slowly to touch the toes. Then hands behind the head and coming up slowly. Repeat each one thirty times. These are strong exercises because the players are using their body weight.

Repetition running:

Pitch length about 100 yards. Jogging first, then sprinting but easing down at about the 70 yard mark. Repeat eight times.

Mark the pitch out with corner flags and another flag in the centre so the players run round the corner flags, across the pitch and round the other corner flags to run in a figure eight. Run in pairs and just a strong run all the way. Not a sprint, not a jog. Just a strong run.

Now running in threes with a ball. Have two players together, one with a ball and the third player about fifty yards away. At a signal the players with a ball set off sprinting with the ball to the far man who takes over the ball and sprints back with it for the third man to repeat. Keep it going for five minutes.

This is designed to help the players feel comfortable running with the ball. Some players always look clumsy with the ball bobbing around their knees while others have a nice touch. Emphasise the importance of keeping the ball weighted just right at their feet so that they could make an instant pass if required.

Sprint session:

With the players in groups of four to provide rest periods each player does two ten-yard sprints to a marker. Then two twenty-yard sprints to another marker followed by two thirty-yard sprints and two forty-yard sprints. We do not take the times but call encouragement to each player to go faster.

Eighth day—Friday

A friendly match against another club.

Afternoon free and with Saturday and Sunday allow the players to recover.

Ninth day—Monday

Morning:

Repetition runs across the pitch. Working in threes, two on one side of the pitch with a ball, one player on the far side. At a signal from the coach one player sprints across the pitch with the ball under close control. At the other side of the pitch the second player takes the ball and sprints back with it for the third player to repeat. Keep this going for ten minutes with the players getting two rest periods while one is working.

Now pair off the players and position on the touchline as base line. One player passes the ball out across the pitch about 15 yards and his partner sprints out to collect it. With the ball the partner turns while the serving player now comes out to offer a challenge while the man with the ball tries to beat him and reach the base line with the ball under control. Break off after 45 seconds and repeat with the players changing roles.

Now organise a six v. six game with conditions if required for thirty minutes.

The other players will practise shooting at goal and heading at goal in groups. Change the groups over with the six v. six players so that all groups work at the three different activities.

Shooting practice: One group serving for the other group to shoot on the volley, half volley and on the turn. Make it competitive by counting the number of successful shots by each group.

Work at this from different angles by varying the angle of the service so that the players shoot from straight in front of goal and from angles when the goalkeeper can come out and narrow the angle.

Vary this by having the servers give the ball in close to goal, thereby calling for quick reaction shooting. Serve at different heights and different angles.

Heading practice at goal at the other end of the pitch. Start with the players in pairs outside the penalty area, one defender and the other an attacker. At a signal from the coach each pair jogs towards goal and when the server gives them a high ball thrown in for accuracy, they compete for the ball with the attacking player trying to score.

Vary this by giving the attacking player a slight advantage by instructing the defending player that he must not move until his opponent does. Server throws the ball and this should just give the attacking player time to get in his header before the defender can reach him.

Afternoon:

After warming up as preferred, sprinting in various forms.

Back to back chasing. Line all the players up, back to back in pairs and number each pair. The coach calls number one and the player nominated to sprint takes off with the player on his back having to turn and try to catch him. In quick succession call out numbers and keep everyone as involved as possible. After twenty to thirty yards each pair returns to original position ready to go again. Halfway through the session change the roles of the pairs.

After this divide the players into groups of four for a forty yard sprint. The first man in each group sprints forty yards and when he arrives the second man takes off. Keep going so that each man does four sprints.

Finish this session off with good thirty yard sprints as individuals running in groups. For example, if you have twenty players there would be two groups of ten. The first group sprints thirty yards to the second group who immediately sprint back. When the second group has sprinted, the first group starts again. Repeat so that each individual player does four thirty-yard sprints with only minimum rest periods in between.

Tenth day—Tuesday

Morning:

Friendly match against another club.

Afternoon . . . free.

Eleventh day—Wednesday

Morning:

After warming up, fifteen minutes spent on ball skills.

Then dribbling practice. Posts set up at intervals on forty yard run. Each player in succession dribbles his ball, first with the right foot between the posts, then sprints straight back with the ball under close control. Repeat with the left foot. Fifteen minutes.

Splitting the players into groups they cross the ball for each other to head at goal, crossing from the right. Change servers with headers. Then repeat with crosses from the left.

Now the players are split into two groups, each having a spell at the following activities:

(a) One against one shooting practice, as explained before with opponent starting one yard behind shooter and trying to catch him.

(b) Centre forward and centre back and right side defence facing attacks from the left side attack. Then change over so that the centre forward attacks with the right side of the attack against the centre back and left side of the defence.

Swimming—twenty minutes.

Afternoon:

Maze runs. Runs with obstacles on a competitive basis by taking the players' times, for about thirty-five minutes.

The players run in and out of posts, under a hurdle, over two hurdles one after the other, round a post and over another hurdle to a marker. In all about sixty yards. Each player does the maze run, then finishes with a strong run straight back.

There would be four different mazes with the hurdles for example in different places just to change the running.

The players would be divided into four groups, each working at one maze run and change so that every group works at each maze run. Each player would do four sprints over each maze.

Twelfth day—Thursday

Morning . . . free.

Afternoon.

Friendly match against another club.

Thirteenth day—Friday

Training morning only. Warm up individually as preferred, then running exercises with twisting, jumping etc. as before.

Small sided games with conditions and finish with a sprint session.

Afternoon . . . free.

By now the players should be fit, but they still need sharpening up for there is a difference between being fit and being match fit.

In recent years Ipswich began to spend a week or so at this stage of their preparations in Holland and we travelled there on the Saturday.

Staying at the Dutch FA training centre at Zeist we can monitor the players food and rest. The players need competitive games but we have to guard against serious injury and at the first sign of a knock we would take the injured player off to prevent aggravation of the injury.

In Holland we played four games, on Monday, Wednesday, Friday and Sunday, all in the evenings. During these games we would try different players and change our team formation, and after the first two games we would think about resting any players not showing their true form.

On match days the players who are not due to play would do quite a hard training session in the morning similar to what we have already done. This would take the form of general fitness work and speed running, as well as work with the ball.

On match days the players due to play would warm up

and then do the usual running, jogging and twisting; turning and running backwards etc. as already explained.

Then we would have a session of three-quarter-pace running followed by competitive running with a partner and finish with some sprints. The players then rest during the afternoon for the game in the evening.

After the matches in Holland our training on rest days would depend on the weaknesses that have been seen in the match the previous evening. This training would be mostly functional with groups of players working at different aspects of the game, perhaps even the whole team in the form of attack against defence in half the pitch.

It should be stressed that all functional work must be done at match pace at this stage or it will have no value. Working at match pace, whatever the objective, is obviously good for general fitness and speed.

We travelled back to Ipswich on the Monday. By now the players were ready for competitive play but during this week we would play three games against teams from lower divisions. The aim now is to build up confidence with good wins and hopefully, lots of goals.

We would continue to train on the days when there was no match but now the emphasis will be on functional training for individuals or sectors of the team, and even the team as a whole.

Our last practice game would be on the Saturday, thus leaving a full week before the first league game for anyone to recover from a minor knock.

Training during the last week of preparation would be similar to the schedule given below for a week in which we had no mid-week game.

It must be stressed of course that clubs at a lower level in both age and status would have to scale down the physical aspect of training to suit their players and our full schedule is given as a guide only.

To demonstrate this, young players who train only once or twice a week will obviously benefit both from sprint work and from longer runs. But young players and amateurs can not be expected to train like professionals.

In these circumstances, once the players have become tired during a training session it will be a good idea to stage some kind of game. It can be small sided if there are not enough players, or a full game if the club has two teams. The important point is that once tired, the players will probably not extend themselves if asked to do more running. But a game of any kind with its built-in competitive spirit will get more out of the players than they would otherwise give.

But even in these circumstances, as the commencement of the league programme approaches the coach should begin to insist on the games being played at match pace. If some of the players are noticed to be "coasting" the coach would be well advised to stop the game and threaten them with more running if the rhythm of the play is not maintained.

On this theme it may be noticed that back players or midfield players will break forward as they would in matches but would then jog back to their customary positions. The coach should insist that when players break forward they must sprint back to take up their usual positions when their attacking move breaks down.

TRAINING DURING THE SEASON
A typical week with no mid-week match:

Monday
Morning:
Light training, for example small sided games with conditions.

Afternoon:
Players under 22 years come back for functional training
—according to playing position.

Tuesday
Morning:
Stamina day. Two hours very hard training.
Afternoon:
Functional training in groups according to positions. Then
finish with speed training and sprints.

Wednesday
Day off for everyone except the goalkeeper who works
with the coach for one hour.

Thursday:
Morning:
Two and a half hours work. After warming up, shooting
practice, functional training and practice at set pieces.
Finish with speed work and sprints.
Afternoon . . . free.

Friday:
Morning:
After warming up, agility exercises and speed work for
one hour. Goalkeeper trains with a coach in a sand pit to
prevent injury before game next day.

Saturday
Game.
A typical week with a mid-week game, usually on
Tuesday evening:

Monday
Morning only:
After warming up, functional training according to
positions. One hour.

Tuesday
   Morning:
Warm up and then short session for speed training and sprints. Goalkeeper trains in sand pit.
   Evening:
Game.

Wednesday
   Free.

Thursday
   Morning:
Warm up and then shooting practices and functional training according to positions.

Friday
   Morning:
Warm up and then speed work and sprints. Practise set pieces.

Saturday
   Game.

10/ The Treatment of Soccer Injuries

by **Fred Street**

Fred Street was born in London on 3rd October 1933 and has spent more than twenty-five years in Physical Training and as a remedial gymnast and physiotherapist. Most of this time was spent working in London hospitals and a National Health Service rehabilitation centre.

For many years he worked with Bertie Mee, later to become Arsenal manager, before spending two years in Melbourne, Australia.

Returning to England, he began work in London once more, continuing to treat injured players from several London professional clubs and in 1968, Stoke City manager, Tony Waddington, invited him to join the club as trainer.

Arsenal brought him back to London in the same capacity in 1971, and since 1974 he has also been the trainer of the full England team.

In continental Europe the trainer is in fact the coach whereas in England the trainer is largely unknown and seen by the public only when he goes onto the pitch to treat an injured player.

The trainer plays a vital part in the set-up of professional clubs, getting injured players fit again, and the author has drawn on long experience in this field to offer advice intended for clubs that do not have expensive equipment nor a qualified physiotherapist.

Knowing that a list of black and white, do's and dont's is both difficult and dangerous, the author offers advice on the treatment of a wide variety of injuries and the section on helping a player back to fitness after a cartilage operation is one of the most important.

This advice however is intended as a guide only and not to be regarded as a substitute for seeking a qualified medical opinion.

BROAD PRINCIPLES

The trainer's aim each week is to provide the manager with as many fit and free from injury players as possible, to make his selection from. This is not only the clear black and white, fit or not fit players, but the fringe grey area of players who are carrying some slight problem but would probably get through a game. The manager needs all that information for his selections so that he can adjust his choice of, for instance, the substitute, if he knows a certain player may not last 90 minutes. This is a particular problem when there are a lot of fixtures, shortage of players, and a lot of injury problems.

To achieve this aim of fit players each Saturday a trainer must treat injuries and maintain the fitness of the injured players as far as possible within the limitations of the injury, a delicate balance between doing too much and aggravating the injury and not doing enough and losing general fitness. Ideally, injured players should do as much training within the limits of the injury, and this should be progressed as the injury subsides and the damage heals until full training is reached, the player is then able to rejoin normal squad training having lost the minimum of general fitness in the minimum of time. As with all ideals it is not practical but that is what we aim at and hope to get as near to as possible. Of course all injuries get better with time, particularly soft tissue sports injuries as the majority are tears and strains, knocks and bruises, and if

players were just given three weeks off the injury would
heal. But then he would need two weeks training, so that
in effect the injury has cost five weeks. By training and
treatment these "running repairs" can be returned to
playing much quicker. There are very few injuries that
prevent a player from doing some training to some degree
after the first forty-eight hours even if it is only body work.
There is a saying that "the treatment room and remedial
gymnasium should not be an escape route from training",
but it should not be a punishment block either. Getting
the best out of people is an art whether it be treatment,
training or playing.

On the pitch

This is where most injuries start, although training pro-
duces a large crop too. Broadly divided into two groups,
injuries are direct and indirect: the direct injury is due to
contact with an opponent or the ball, and the indirect
injuries are muscle pulls and strains as a result of tissues
giving way under stress, hamstrings, calf muscles and
groin strains.

Treatment on the pitch is very limited and boils down
to a quick assessment of whether a player can carry on or
not. Your main guides under these conditions are seeing
what happened, if you are lucky, and any information you
can get from the player, not usually the best witness under
the circumstances of the heat of the moment. As a rough
guide I have found that if the player is more concerned
about being fouled and complaining to the referee it is a
fair bet that it is a transient knock which will pass off in a
few moments. If he is preoccupied with the pain then it is
worthy of more attention and you may have to take him
to the sidelines for a closer look. Open cuts and bleeding
noses are easily recognised and must be assessed as to the
need for a stitch with cuts and whether a bleeding nose is

broken or not. If a player is knocked out or very still when you reach him try not to move him at all until you feel around any area you saw hit or until the player comes round. Use smelling salts sparingly and even then not close up to the nostrils as this makes the player jerk his head away and may cause further damage.

The majority of incidents are passing and the player carries on, and will usually let you know if it is getting worse. Broadly speaking direct knocks carry on, and are all right during the game but usually stiffen up after. Slight pulls of muscles and strained joint ligaments run worse and usually the player comes off. They are broad guides and there is a wide variation within that outline depending upon the player and the trainer's knowledge of him and his reaction to injury. Some make a lot of fuss, others need protection from themselves.

Most common injuries

Most trainers would probably agree that the most common injuries are the bruised thigh muscle which players refer to as a "dead leg" and the sprained ankle where the foot has rolled over, which can result in a minor "tweak" of the joint with minimal damage to the ligaments or a full blown sprain with damage to the ligaments and capsule of the joint and even slight bone damage.

All damage to tissues causes some bleeding, some swelling, some heat, and some pain. Some or all of these signs are present in varying degrees and the sum total causes loss of function. Immediate treatment is attention to the recognition and control of these symptoms, and early diagnosis with the club doctor is essential. Bone damage is either confirmed or excluded by X-ray although in the case of hair line cracks it is not always definite. Ice-packs, elevation of the limb in question, pressure by strapping, and rest with anti-inflammatory and pain-killing tablets from the doctor will control the symptoms for the first thirty-six to forty-eight hours, after which time it is possible to take a closer look at the area and start mobilising and strengthening as far as symptoms allow.

Ice packs

These are a useful "instant" treatment for swelling following a direct knock, for instance a kick on the shin with a resulting local swelling or bump. In conjunction with cold soaks or running cold water they are very effective in controlling and sometimes reducing this local swelling before applying some form of compression to keep the swelling under control.

The packs can be bought ready made or easily made up yourself. The ready made are particularly useful when playing away, as they can be applied whilst travelling home in the coach or train. They are easy to store and carry and as they are sealed cause no mess. They consist of a sachette with two separate compartments containing chemicals which when mixed by removing a divider create a liquid with a low temperature. The whole thing can then be held or bandaged against the swollen area. They are not expensive, especially if reserved for use only when travelling, as the same effect can be produced at next to no cost playing at home, with towels and crushed ice.

Very simple effective ice packs can be made with ice cubes from the fridge crushed and laid in a damp towel, then folded over and again laid or bandaged onto the swollen area. Both these applications should only be applied for a maximum of ten minutes, followed by a period of rest with the limb in elevation, and then perhaps a second application of ice before applying pressure to the part.

Elevation

A term often seen used, e.g. exercise in elevation, or elevate the leg before applying the bandage. This simply means raising the level of the legs above the body so that gravity will assist the return flow of blood and fluids to the body. With the player or patient lying flat on his back, put a support such as pillows under the legs so that they are about 30 to 45 degrees to the body, and the effect of that simple action for about half an hour can be quite dramatic on tissues which are distended with fluids from a kick in say, the calf. If this is done before applying any pressure bandage, the effect of the bandage is greater.

A more continuous form of elevation is raising the foot of the player's bed overnight just a few inches, say the thickness of two telephone books. This helps to avoid the stagnation of fluids in areas around the lower leg and ankle. A practical example of the effect of gravity is when a player has had a knock which appears minor at the time, and during the evening he may be sitting with his foot down at a cinema, and at the end of the evening has a fat ankle. This of course should be avoided by support and instructions to players with knocks to literally "put their feet up".

A typical injury—haematoma thigh (dead leg)

Most commonly occurs when an opponent's knee hits a player in mid-thigh causing the thigh to feel numb with transient loss of function (hence the players' nickname). Attention on the field is limited to easing the instant pain as far as possible, the cold spray has a slight effect, plus getting the player to brace his thigh muscle and then bend the knee. Presuming it is not too bad and the player carries on, he will probably function quite well throughout the game whilst he is hot, and it is only later that he will tighten and stiffen.

It is probably preferable that after the game a player with this type of injury has a shower and not a hot soak. On examination there will be a diffuse area of tenderness on the front of the thigh corresponding to the blow. The stiffness of the muscle and limitation of knee joint movement will not be apparent unless you lie the player face down and bend the knee, only then are the muscles concerned on the stretch, and it will be easy to compare the limited range of movement with the good leg. Having decided that this is a haematoma thigh without underlying bone damage, the thigh should be wrapped in wet towels and crushed ice for about ten minutes; then firmly strap the thigh overnight with instructions to rest and elevate the leg, even perhaps to raise the foot of the bed a few inches. It may seem obvious but players are people and they need to be told not to go out dancing or to the cinema and so on that evening. The strapping and ice may be repeated and re-applied next day, but it is debatable as to whether bringing players in for treatment on Sunday morning causes more irritation to the site of injury than the treatment is worth, far better to visit the player at home.

After two days or so the area will be less diffuse with localised tenderness, and symptoms will be considerably reduced, and a stretching routine can be started, as well as gentle heat. Heat can be applied without the need for expensive machines or lamps. Hot wet towels, hot soaks, are within the range of all clubs, and are very comforting and easing as a preparation for stretching the affected area. With the player lying face down, gently bend the knee as if to bring the heel against the back of the thigh. This should be done gently and slowly into the area of pain and then away. Little and often is the order of the day. Do not use pressure, let the player "feel" his way, and do not massage the tender area on the front of the thigh, as this will only irritate the area.

Range of movement will progress slowly day to day, and some other activities can be carried out without causing any problems or hindering recovery. Circuit training, including half squats, abdominals, and even light jogging with a low back lift action will be possible sometimes within ten days. No ball work should be allowed or attempted, and no sprinting until such time as an equal range of pain free muscle extensibility and knee movement are found on clinical examination, and even then it will be noted that on running the player will run with a low back lift of his leg which must be eradicated before being passed fit to play.

Fitness testing for this injury as with all injuries should be to test and not to destroy. It is quite easy to over test, dead ball kicking for instance . . . a player may not hit more than ten dead balls in a game, so that to test him hitting fifty such balls would be wrong. For this injury, pain free ability to sprint, hit a ball then sprint again, change direction, run with a normal action of back lift, and pass a clinical examination on the treatment table, should satisfy you and, more important, the player that he is fit to play.

That is a very broad general outline of a typical injury, which could cover anything from ten days to six weeks depending upon the severity of the original damage, but the principles remain constant.

The more serious injuries and conditions such as fractures, operative procedures to remove torn cartilage, and operations to repair ligaments are of course subject to the control of the surgeon but the procedures of building muscle and mobilising joints are the same, and progressive training as and when players are allowed to take weight on fractures continues, and a considerable amount of work like circuit training can be done even in plaster cast from toe to hip.

Whilst these sort of injuries and the daily problems of sore throats, headaches, ingrowing toenails, dental appointments make up the meat of a trainer's day, it is preparation for the game and selected players that take priority on match day. At the professional level this may include an overnight stay at an hotel the night before the game, so that attention to meals comes into the trainer's responsibility. Some players do not travel well or do not sleep well in hotels, and they must be looked after with various medications.

On match day most players take a light meal at around 11.30 a.m. that consists of light easily digestible and convertible food such as tea, toast, cornflakes, and maybe a poached egg on toast. Some players like a little chocolate, others toast and honey. It is difficult to be hard and fast about pre-match meals as so much tradition and personal preference colours the issue.

Preparing players for the match between 2 p.m. and kick-off at 3 p.m. is a ritual routine that the trainer plays an important role in. At this time players are in their most vulnerable and suggestible state as they prepare for the game before them. It is a time of stress and test for them, and they need support. Support that the staff should provide in whatever way they are qualified to do.

Strappings for ankles, oil massage for the legs, a word of re-assurance for a player who has just recovered from injury that he will be all right.

Anything and everything that a player needs should be available to the players on arrival at the dressing room. Kit laid out, boots clean, and newly laced with correct studs for ground conditions. Plenty of towels and baths ready for those who like a hot soak before a game, and staff must have time for the idiosyncrasies that players display, such as a special bit of tape around a toe, or camphorated oil on the chest, or making a fuss about shorts being too big or too small. It is all about getting players out on the field feeling ready to play with nothing irritating them no matter how small.

This should carry over to the field of play, not only should the trainer be looking out for injury or physical problems, but also if players need anything, a tie-up for a loose stocking, a shin guard, loose stud, goalkeepers' gloves etc. Consequently the trainer's bag has a supply of kit as well as medical needs. A pair of pliers are as likely to be called for as scissors.

After the game, apart from the known injuries, all knocks and bruises, cuts and grazes should be examined and dressed. Anyone who has been knocked out, however briefly, should see the doctor. Having drinks available at half time and full time are routine responsibilities, and drinks on the line just in case of extra time in cup ties sometimes gets overlooked.

Keep notes and records of all the players, plus an annual medical. Up to date inoculations, chest X-rays, weight and height. Note players weaknesses, in particular the young player who may have some adolescent condition that could be aggravated by some of the normal training.

Diagnosis on the pitch

Not ideal conditions to diagnose under but if a cut is pouring with blood or a leg is bent where it should be straight then you don't need a lot of knowledge to see what is wrong.

Fortunately the majority of injuries are not that serious and most are transient knocks that players recover from in a few moments and carry on with the game. A closer look can be taken at half time or full time.

The injuries that cause most concern are the doubtful ones, where a player carries on after a few minutes' attention either on the pitch or the sideline, but continues to hobble. These and the head injuries with blurred vision etc., you cannot take a chance with.

Broadly speaking the direct knocks and bruises can usually carry on whilst indirect injuries such as strains, sprains, pulled muscles, will get worse the longer they carry on.

With deep cuts, stitching is essential and the sooner the better. There are products on the market for holding the edges of a cut together until such time as a stitch or two can be put in.

After the game, head injuries, in particular where a player has been knocked out, however briefly, should be seen by a doctor, or taken to a local casualty department, as should injuries to eyes and ears. Remember also a ball in the face which made the nose bleed is a head injury and should be treated as such. When in doubt, take no chances, especially with head injuries and with suspected leg fractures. Just make the player comfortable, and send for the ambulance or doctor. I know doing nothing sounds negative, but in limited circumstances it is best.

Run of the mill cuts, grazes, and abrasions that every player has after every game should be seen and cleaned with a soluble antiseptic and covered with a clean elastoplast dressing. There are some non-stick dressings available on the market for grass-burn type grazes that "weep" quite badly. Goalkeepers suffer from these on hard grounds, in particular on the bony points of the hip joint.

Cartilage problems
For the club without a qualified physiotherapist, a

player recovering from a cartilage operation will present a problem for to train too early or too much, causes swelling and pain, while to rest too much wastes the muscles of the leg.

A torn cartilage is probably the most common of the serious injuries that a soccer player can suffer and it is worthwhile therefore to devote special attention to it here.

There are two cartilages in each joint, one on each side, forming a buffer between the two bones which make up the knee joint. They can be torn or dislodged, and it would appear that soccer provides stresses that give rise to their damage more than most sports although it is not uncommon in skaters, skiers and any high level of activity that puts a lot of demand on the knee, of rotation and flexion.

It is possible to damage a cartilage suddenly all in one go as it were, with one incident, or to have a troublesome knee which gives a history of small problems over a period of time. It would be a very rare occasion to go on to a player on the pitch and make an instant diagnosis of cartilage trouble. Diagnosis is more often based on a series of incidents each one giving more evidence leading to the suspicion of a torn cartilage upon which the orthopeadic surgeon will confirm the suspicion by deciding to operate and remove the torn cartilage.

Any or all of the following signs and symptoms may be present at once or over a period.

1. Locking of the joint, in any point of its range.
2. Swelling of the joint.
3. Pain.
4. Wasting of the muscles of the joint (Quadriceps).
5. Inability to lock the joint straight (a form of locking).
6. Inability to take weight onto a full knees bend.
7. On examination, producing a "clunk" from the knee joint.

In the absence of any other reason to support these symptoms there is a strong chance that a torn cartilage exists. These signs may not be there all the time and indeed the player may have periods when all seems OK. From what I have said you will gather that diagnosis of this particular condition is far from easy and most surgeons want considerable evidence before proceeding with operative procedure. Indeed unless very conclusive symptoms and history are presented, the player is often told to go back and get on with playing in a make or break effort.

In the event that a cartilage is torn, it is removed, and rehabilitation back to full playing fitness is started the day after the operation. Progress is usually continuous unless complications or other problems were found to be present at operation. But for the straightforward case, which is the majority, it is between six and eight weeks before the player is fit to play competitive soccer. You may read of players playing in as little as three, but this is rare and questionable, the test is not how soon the player played but did he keep playing regularly. To come back early and miss every other game is only limited success. Playing a little later but staying playing is preferable.

Rehabilitation following removal of cartilage

More often than not it is the inside cartilage which has caused the trouble so that a small crescent-shaped incision is visible just inside and alongside the kneecap. The player would be in hospital approximately a week to ten days, and depending on the surgeon's preference the leg will be in a pressure bandage or plaster cylinder.

The player is of course under the surgeon, and who does what and when will depend upon your relationship to the surgeon and your club facilities. But should you have a player in your care following such an operation, he will probably be with you after three weeks or so when he is being allowed to do some activity to build up his muscles in the thigh. Controlled strong hard exercise for the thighs without the pounding of running and twisting, should build muscle without causing swelling of the knee. Squats and step up exercises within the limit of the knee movement are excellent in meeting these problems of building muscle without irritation of the knee. To incorporate these exercises into circuit training, thereby keeping some general level of fitness up as well, is the best of both worlds. Unless the knee swells or is painful, the amount of muscle work should be high, and the player should work hard. Daily examination of the knee should be routine and any problems should be reported and assessed, but the general trend should be towards more and harder work, with any fresh activity such as the introduction of running only undertaken with the approval and knowledge of the surgeon. Ball work should be left until a high level of athletic fitness is achieved without symptoms from the knee, and even then introduced gently and sparingly. By the time a player plays it should be more a proof of fitness than a fitness test.

STRAPPINGS

Strappings to support joints or to control swellings must be applied carefully and with instructions to the player. Many players like to play in strappings, particularly of the ankles, and whilst it is not to be encouraged it is a fact, so that it might as well be done properly if it is to be done at all.

Strappings can either be 3 inch wide elastoplast or 4 inch crêpe for the ankle which I feel is the only joint which can be strapped effectively enough to play with and provide a degree of support, so I will only deal with the ankle. If the knee joint really needs a strapping then the player should not be playing at all.

Strapping an ankle for playing

Players who have recently recovered from a sprained ankle feel happier about playing if the ankle is supported by a figure of eight elastoplast strapping, and others like a strapping to protect the ankle from the superficial cuts and grazes that this area is subject to. The tightness is very much an individual thing. Too tight can cause cramp under the foot, and lack of mobility, too loose and there is not a lot of point in the strapping. Firm pressure from just behind the toes to about four inches above the ankle leaving no gaps is a broad view. Strap with foot in mid position with the strapping pulling the foot upwards and outwards.

Strapping following injury

Most common for ankle and knee joints, and for thigh injury. Strappings are applied for support and comfort and rest of the damaged tissues. A knee or ankle that has been diagnosed as a torn ligament or whatever needs to be supported and immobilised for a period of say twenty-four hours after which a closer look is possible when initial pain and tenderness has settled a little.

Pressure bandage or support needs to be firm and large, extending well above and below the site of injury, and should consist of a layer of cotton wool followed by broad firmly applied crêpe bandage. Make sure pressure is even and no edges of the bandage cut in. The leg should be elevated as described earlier, and overnight, and the player told to control his activity. Care should be taken to avoid the bandage being too tight and causing blood flow to be cut off. If the player experiences numbness or pins and needles or extreme throbbing pain, he should remove the strapping and not leave it on just because you put it on!

It is probably cheapest to use crêpe bandages for strapping as they are washable and can be used repeatedly. Washing in fact returns some of the elasticity to them. For ankles the best size is 4 inch and for knees and thighs 6 inch.